THE RETURN TO LAISSER FAIRE

SIR ERNEST BENN

THE RETURN TO LAISSER FAIRE

THE FOUNDATION OF PROSPERITY

By ERNEST J. P. BENN

D. APPLETON & COMPANY

NEW YORK   MCMXXIX

Printed in Great Britain by Ebenezer Baylis & Son, Ltd., The Trinity Press,
Worcester.

CONTENTS

CHAPTER   PAGE

I   INTRODUCTORY   -   -   -   -   -   9

II   GOOD AND BAD GOVERNMENT   -   -   23

III   MERRIE ENGLAND -   -   -   -   -   34

IV   PRODUCTION VERSUS POVERTY   -   -   44

V   DELAYS AND RESTRICTIONS   -   -   -   56

VI   ETHICS AND ECONOMICS   -   -   -   66

VII   THE LIMITATIONS OF MONEY   -   -   78

VIII THE BLESSING OF COMPETITION   -   -   91

IX   THE REAL CAUSE OF UNEMPLOYMENT   -   103

X   THE BURDEN OF BUREAUCRATS   -   -   114

XI   EDUCATION AS A VITAL FORCE   -   -   126

XII   HOUSING   -   -   -   -   -   -   137

XIII ATTEMPTS AT SOCIALISM   -   -   -   153

XIV   SUPPLY AND DEMAND   -   -   -   -   165

XV   COMBINES AND PROFITS   -   -   -   172

XVI   CONTROL AND LIBERTY -   -   -   -   185

XVII PRIVATE WEALTH AND PUBLIC INTEREST   198

XVIII THE INDIVIDUALIST AS A POLITICIAN   -   211

CHAPTER I

INTRODUCTORY

THE history of England for eight or nine centuries is the story of the struggle of man to be free. One after another the powers over life and liberty have been broken, at last real democracy has been achieved, and thirty million votes each possess an equal value and an equal power to direct the affairs of the commonwealth. The first and natural tendency, in this new situation, is to use the new found power to oppress and suppress, for all through the ages most power has been used that way. Just as a newly appointed policeman is naturally anxious to lock up his first man, so a newly founded democracy is over-anxious to make its presence in the world obvious and evident.

In the age-long advocacy of the vote, virtues have been attributed to it which it does not possess, and evils which have nothing to do with it have been blamed on its absence. But as with the policeman so with the democratic power, age and experience will teach the wisdom of waiting round the corner or on the other side of the street, until there is at least a reasonable probability that the interposition of authority may be useful, and is more likely to reduce than to increase the commotion or the trouble.

From the days of primitive tyrants to the days of civilised autocrats, the individual man has been the bond slave of the State. Can it therefore be wondered at, that having become the master of the

9

State, he is prone to consider that institution as something in the nature of a bond slave to him. Hence there have arisen numerous and recurring attempts usually labelled " social reform " to make the State provide various forms of sustenance for its citizens.   Ever since there was a vote it has been used to " house the working classes," to make the miners life a comfortable one, to provide employment and generally to abolish poverty.   This movement, slow at first but constantly increasing in ignorance and strength, has reached its zenith in demagogues like Mr. Lloyd George and Mr. Winston Churchill who openly and unashamed offer benefits in exchange for votes, and have so far been able to gain increasing power by blaming the widespread poverty which their quackery produces upon the remnants of sanity that remain with us.

Democracy is also going through the troubles of infancy and adolescence in other ways.   With the popular vote the people imagine themselves to be all powerful, but the use of the vote for economic and other purposes to which it is both unsuitable and ineffective, is rapidly shifting the powers and liberties, won at such cost by the people from the autocratic tyrant, to a new class of oppressor more numerous, more secure and, being impersonal, more objectionable, the bureaucratic tyrant.

We have yet to learn how to apply the Individualism which secured for us liberty and freedom, to the proper and effective use of those blessings.   In the meantime we are the victims of a wave of Collectivism which having rolled far up the shore of civilisation is now happily and naturally on the ebb.

The revival of Individualism will be the outstanding characteristic of the second quarter of the twentieth century. All competent observers are, to some extent at least, agreed about that, and there are at least two good reasons why this prediction should be regarded in the nature rather of a scientific forecast, like a modern weather report, than of mere political prophecy.

There is, first of all, that inexorable arbiter of human affairs called a pendulum, which would sweep us back from all the Socialism and Collectivism of the last two or three decades, even if Socialism and Collectivism were, in fact, the blessings which their apostles claim them to be.

But the swing of the pendulum will be helped and accelerated in this case by the proven weaknesses of the other course. Individualism as a cause is already firmly established amongst us, although the movement which bears that name is barely a couple of years old. Individualism is a protest against the modern way of looking at things social and political. It doubts the divine wisdom of the mass; it questions the acceptance of the herd instinct as a safe guide to political perfection; it denies the doctrine of the infallibility of the committee.

Union is undoubtedly strength when warlike purposes are afoot, but the application of the proverb to every peaceful purpose is now questioned. *Vox populi suprema lex* may be a true proverb, it is con-

ceivable that the will of the people should be regarded as the highest law, but it is of the gravest
import into what way of thinking the people has
been guided by its leaders and teachers. People
in the mass are notoriously lazy-minded and leave
most of their thinking to be done for them by others;
hence the power of the Press and of stunt-creators
in general. It is therefore our endeavour in this
book to put before them a better alternative to the
present commonly accepted doctrine that no man
may do an act or think a thought until it has the
sanction or the backing of some conference,
council, committee, union, association, society, or
soviet.

Students of the English language will in later
years discover that about the beginning of the year
1927 the word " Individualism " reappeared in the
English vocabulary. For a year or more prior to
that a little group of political " discontents " met on
several occasions to discuss ways and means of dealing with the Collectivist mania then and now sweeping through human affairs. The problem was how
to revive that sense of personal pride which
threatened to desert the English character, of which
it is the most precious part, and without which the
glorious history of Britain and of the British Empire
would not have been written.

That little group, of which I was a member, hesi-
tated long and thoughtfully before adopting the
word " Individualist " as a label. Strange as it
may seem to-day, some of us demurred only as
recently as two years ago even to breathe the word.

It was objected against it that it was harsh, hard, materialistic, out of keeping with the popular notions of service and citizenship, and it was solemnly predicted that any movement so ticketed would be doomed to failure from the start. We played with "Freedom," "Liberty," "Prosperity," "Life," and "Liberalism," and many other symbols of our dominant thought were mooted. Then we took our courage in both hands, and, in spite of warnings that would have deterred men whose convictions were not so deeply rooted and unshakable, plumped for "Individualism."

There are few who can now doubt that the word is destined once more in our history to serve as a weapon of victory, of victory over the forces and influences making for disruption and disintegration in our national life.

From the Prime Minister downwards few politicians can to-day make a speech without some reference to Individualism. The political leader writer finds himself under the same necessity. The report of the Liberal Industrial Inquiry devotes a whole chapter to misrepresenting the aims of Individualists. Individualism is once more a live issue with us. It holds out new hope to a State-ridden world, and has brought a patch of blue into the Collectivist-cloud-obscured sky.

Individualism can be considered in various ways. As a philosophy it seems to me to offer the only chance of satisfaction. I am not of those who consider the real aim of life to be happiness, if by happiness is meant wealth, idleness, something for nothing, absence of effort. But if the aim of life is happiness and contentment derived from duty done, then, I argue, through Individualism alone can such an end be reached.

Religion, of course, is and must always be essentially individualistic. No Heaven that I have ever heard of contained a committee. Individualism as a basis of government is, as I shall hope to show, the only basis upon which the ideal State can be erected. A citizenship which is actuated by Individualism will wash its hands of that " citizenship by proxy " which is variously called social reform, Socialism and Communism. All these shibboleths mean paying somebody else with other people's money to do your duty as a citizen. In the Individualist State each citizen does his own duty—a very different thing.

Individualism as the foundation of a system of economics presents the only prospect of wealth for all. With every individual striving to contribute his utmost to the common stock, the condition of society improves and the standard of living rises. What a contrast to the Collectivist-ruled world where everyone is tempted to deplete the common stock, and society sinks to ever lower standards!

The Individualist is, of course, opposed to Socialism, and he is, therefore, called upon to support every anti-Socialist movement. Political organisation, whether Conservative or Liberal, is full of anti-Socialist societies, all of which are quite good in their way. Much personal satisfaction, however, is not to be derived from a purely " anti " attitude of any kind. Only to be an anti-Socialist is not good enough for a self-respecting person, and that is why we preach the gospel of Individualism.

The economic battle has for too long been waged on ground chosen by the enemy: the present position reflects little credit upon Individualists and those who think as we do. Some fantastic doctrinaire, lacking in all qualifications for the purpose, propounds a scheme unassociated with precedent or experience, and at once all sorts and classes of sensible people find themselves drawn into a discussion which has no real foothold in common sense, in human experience, in fact or in practice.

And yet the foolish theorist is able to control the platform and keep us all busy debating his eccentricities. The bankruptcy of modern politics is in no way better shown than by the fact that the first claim of the other parties to support is that they are anti-Socialist. It is impossible to throw mud without soiling one's own fingers, and so, while modern politicians are busy rejecting Socialism and denouncing its follies, even the Conservatives find themselves left with a trifling bill of £300,000,000 a year on account of pensions, doles and other forms of public assistance.

The mud adheres still more noticeably to the modern Liberals, who now bring out an industrial policy stolen complete from the Socialists while piously protesting in every other paragraph that they will never defile themselves with Socialist doctrine.

Modern Liberalism may be described as the illegitimate offspring of Socialism.

War, perforce, made us all Socialists. In modern war there is no place for Individualism, which is essentially the gospel of peace. War arises from the undue glorification of the State. The State, when it is the servant of the individual, does not go to war. The State which, like the Kaiser-ridden Germany, the system-ridden Russia or the force-ridden Italy, claims the soul of the individual cannot avoid war. So perhaps we have some excuse for the Collectivist distemper which still clings to us and holds us back from real peace.

The challenge of Individualism is, however, making people think, and when the next General Election comes a very large proportion of the voters will have reached the mental stage in which they can clearly see the two alternatives which face us. Are we to continue the pitiful attempt to erect a State whose sole object is to act as wet-nurse to the people, sparing them the painful necessity of doing anything for themselves, or are we to develop a people who can support and look after themselves as well as the State?

"We are unlearning," said the Prime Minister at Bewdley, " the war-time habit of looking to the Government to do everything for us. The Government can lead, guide, help, watch the finances, maintain the defences, but it cannot do the work that the individual has to do for himself to work out his own salvation, and if I have helped in any way, however feeble, to get that into people's heads I shall not have lived in vain, because it is that creed, burnt into the bones of Englishmen, that made this country what it has been, and it is only that creed in practice that will enable us in the future to get the country where we all want to keep it, namely, at the top and in the front.''

There was a time when candidates for Parliamentary honours were under the necessity of bribing the electors with their own money. That has all been altered, and now we have the sorry spectacle of Parliamentary candidates bribing the electors with other people's money. So long as the electors remain under the mistaken impression that the money comes from a few wealthy taxpayers, so long will the trick be effective, but as soon as electors realise that they themselves are paying the money with which they are bribed, then it will cease to work.

We must get our politics back to questions of principle. There never was such widespread interest in citizenship as exists to-day, yet there never was a time when the principles of citizenship were less discussed and less understood. We fail to see the wood for the trees. We must step back from all the details of rival policies and strive to think about those great underlying principles upon which alone a successful society and the good life can be established.

This is where Individualism comes in. There are two distinct ways of approaching the problem of good government. You can look upon the forty odd millions of human beings who inhabit these

2

islands as a helpless mass of ignorance, and there is something to be said for that view. You can decide that they must be regulated, restrained, ordered, restricted, directed and generally provided for. You can reach the conclusion that they do not know how to house themselves, how to find work for themselves, how to provide for their daily needs, or prepare for their old age, and you can decide that these things must be done through the authority of the State.

That is the Socialist, the Collectivist, view. It is a degrading view, because it is based upon the inherent inefficiency of the mass. It is an illogical view, because it assumes that wisdom, which is lacking in the individual, will be found in the citizens in the mass.

As against all this the Individualist approaches considerations of government, the problem of providing the good life and the question of the duties of citizenship, from the other end. Individualism says that either good or bad in the world can only function through the individual, and can function best in a state of liberty. Restraint, regulation, restriction, and all the machinery of government should, therefore, be applied only to the bad. In this manner the maximum of good will prevail. As Cowper puts it:

> " 'Tis liberty alone
> Which gives the flower of fleeting life its sweetness
>   and perfume,
> And we are weeds without it.
> All restraint except what wisdom lays on evil men
> Is evil."

Government is a negative force. The machinery of government can act most easily as a restraining or preventative force, but cannot of itself do much that is constructive. So that, while committees with attendant policemen can make arrangements to restrain pickpockets, Collectivist bodies with accompanying bureaucrats cannot make arrangements to produce wealth.

Thus we get back to principles. We begin to see more clearly the line of cleavage between the Individualist point of view and Collectivist opinion. The former would limit the functions of government to restraining that which is bad, while the latter hopes to use government to produce that which is good.

A further line of cleavage can be clearly drawn. Government can be productive of good in such a realm as education, in some departments of health, and in various other ways which have nothing directly to do with the production of material wealth. But all experience of all time so far proves that when government attempts to make things, to produce things, to create wealth, it fails. Government can create conditions under which the individual is able to function to the fullest advantage. Beyond that it is practically powerless and, in the main, inefficient.

The aim therefore which I have in writing this book is to get politics back to principles. I am not concerned as to whether a pension should be 5s., or 10s., or 15s.—the type of petty argument in which the parties now-a-days are involved. I am concerned with the principles underlying any pension, whatever its size. Individualism says that you cannot pension anybody unless everybody is determined to do his best to do without a pension.

Individualism says that the State cannot find employment for anybody unless everybody makes a resolute effort to find work for himself, relying on the State only in the last resource. Individualism rejects, not merely as absurd and degrading but as dangerous and destructive, the theory so sedulously preached by politicians that the State of itself can provide. The peril which menaces us owing to the growing sense of dependence is enormous, and can never be removed until we have developed in the breast of everyone the old spirit of Individualism and independence.

We will have no more of mere anti-Socialism—that is to flatter the Socialists. We will have Individualism as a constructive system of life, a philosophy of government. Christianity is not recommended to us on the ground that it is anti-heathen; and Individualism must be looked upon as a creed, as a thing which stands by itself, has an existence of its own, anxious to be free from the folly, the stupidity, the meanness of other theories.

Popular education has developed a healthy discontent with things as they are, a discontent which is the very seed of future advancement, but a discontent which is not yet wise enough, not yet sufficiently enlightened, to resist the bait of political maniacs who, with the gift of the gab or the power of the pen, offer new systems designed ostensibly to bring nearer the millennium, but destined, if accepted, to cause the ruin of millions of innocent but credulous people. There has never yet been any serious effort to educate the people in the why and wherefore of the existing state of things. Criticism of slums, criticism of poverty, criticism of unnecessary inequalities is good if accompanied by a knowledge of the manner in which houses are built, the manner in which wealth is made, the manner in which trade is conducted. But criticism, like most Socialist criticism, founded upon complete and utter ignorance of these processes, is full of danger and pregnant with disaster. Such criticism has produced the present political chaos.

In this book my endeavour will be to do two things for the benefit of students of politics and citizenship. I shall set myself out to discredit Socialism, but that is the least worthy and the least inspiring of my aims. I shall do it, if I succeed, not so much by a study and analysis of Socialism, as by a study and explanation of the working of economic laws and the structure of civilised society —the study, in a word, of the science of civilisation and Individualism. I shall write without reference to political party programmes, without reference to election results, and with a sole desire to abide by principles.

My earnest hope is that these pages will be read by that great mass of serious, perplexed electors eager only for the right, unconcerned with party

labels, but much concerned to see this old country
take its proper place once more at the head of the
civilised nations of the world. " The worth of a
State, in the long run, is the worth of the individuals
composing it."

CHAPTER II

GOOD AND BAD GOVERNMENT

GOVERNMENT means, or should mean, the right ordering of all. Modern government has degenerated into tinkering with the wants or rights or liberties of classes or sections or groups, and it is rare, in these days, to hear a political discussion which takes adequate account of the interests of the whole of the community.

The problem before statesmen and other serious citizens is, as Adam Smith puts it, how to arrange that there shall be a " plentiful subsistence " for the 43,000,000 people who inhabit Great Britain. In approaching that problem there are two big general facts to be borne in mind. The first is the fact that during the Victorian era, notwithstanding all the blemishes on the social life of the time, notwithstanding all its shortcomings, all its faults, so widely advertised to-day, that period did provide in this island a better subsistence for the people than had ever been provided before, or had ever been provided in any other country.

Then follows the second big fact, and it is a disquieting one, that to-day there are other countries in which there is a better subsistence for the people as a whole than we are able to provide here. We have sunk relatively in the matter of the general standard of living to a second or third position.

Keeping these two facts in mind, we can approach the problem of providing a plentiful subsistence for the population of Britain in two distinct ways. We can look at the people of the country in the Indi-

vidualist way and think rather of the possibilities
and the powers of each of them, as individuals, or
we can look at them in the more fashionable Collectivist way, and think chiefly of their powers as a
State or a community. Just as there are prevailing
winds so there are prevailing opinions. Society at
any given time has a tendency to look at things in a
given way, and there is always a public mind at work
in one direction or another. If we analyse this great
mind of the public, which for thirty or forty years
has been thinking in the Collectivist way, and
attempt to write a recipe for its composition, giving
the constituent thoughts that make it up, we find
several easily distinguishable elements.

It consists of five main conclusions, all of which,
I suggest, are entirely wrong. It begins with the
general assumption that these 43,000,000 people are
a hopeless mass of ignorance—the view of Carlyle
that they are " mostly fools." There is, of course,
much to be said for that point of view; it is a view
that can be argued; it may even have some truth in
it, but it is the most hopeless and helpless point of
view when held by statesmen or as a philosophy of
government.

Observe the way in which it works out to-day.
We need not select more than half-a-dozen of the
scores of examples that are available. This great
public mind decides that these 43,000,000 people
cannot arrange their own work and so establishes
for their benefit a Ministry of Labour. It further
decides that we are no judges of our own food, so
we must have a Food Council. Then we cannot be

trusted with our own health, so a Ministry of Health is set up. This mass is incapable of finding shelter, so in every district housing officials must be appointed. It cannot cultivate the land satisfactorily, we have therefore to spend millions on heaven-sent institutions like the Ministry of Agriculture. It does not export the right goods to the right markets, consequently it must have a Department of Overseas Trade. It is, as we now learn, no judge of a film, and some appropriate department must therefore be established to put that right. That is, in a broad way, what the public mind is thinking, or is asked to think, to-day.

Whatever may be the theory of the matter, the facts are unfortunate for the supporters of the Collectivist point of view. In the year 1913-14, in pursuance of the policy dictated by the prevailing opinion of the State mind, we spent the sum of £83,000,000 on such services as I have mentioned. In 1926-7, for the same sort of services, we spent £311,400,000. Yet it is undeniable that as our expenditure in all those respects has increased, so the results that we hoped to obtain have diminished.

Turning to the second assumption upon which the public mind works, we find it to be the belief that by diligent search persons can be found free from all the ignorance shown by the mass, who can be put into positions of authority where they may direct the rest in the better performance of their proper functions. That is the theory of the matter, and Individualists may recall with profit the forecast of Herbert Spencer, who, in " Man Versus the State," some sixty years ago, wrote the most remarkable prophecy of the position as it actually exists to-day. I venture to assert that in practice all that we accomplish is a scramble by persons with influence, of one kind or another, to invent jobs for people who fear to test their qualities in the open market.

The third assumption, again wrong, is that when such persons have been placed in positions of authority, the people as a whole will respond to their leadership. Two hundred years ago Montesquieu told us that one of the dangers of organised society was that people were led continually to desire the advantages of society without any of the burdens of it.

This statement is proved over and over again. When you appoint officials, people are tempted to forget their personal responsibility and to leave the struggle for existence in the hands of those who profess to know all about it. In the great public mind there follows next the assumption, again, as I suggest, wrong, that when the officials have been found they will do their jobs. It is far from any wish of mine to write a word of disrespect or show any lack of appreciation of the Civil Service on the personal side, and I hope I shall never be guilty of doing so. But it does seem to me impossible to do a job which from its nature cannot be done.

Many kinds of work cannot be well done without the stimulus of competition, or where there is no real necessity to give satisfaction. Good work may often become impossible when it is free from any real penalties in the event of failure. Let us look for a moment at the matter in a simple and homely way. Take possibly the best of the Civil Servants, the panel doctors, and let us go to tea with a panel doctor's wife. That is a useful way of getting at the real situation—to talk to a man's wife.

Just imagine what she is really thinking and the order of importance in which she, good soul, places her husband's functions. What is her first thought? That he should draw his fees from the benevolent State. Her second thought is that he should look after his private practice, and her third that he should give due consideration to the complicated business of endeavouring to understand official procedure and take his due share in the agitation to get better terms and better conditions. When these three things are properly attended to the panel doctor's wife is prepared to consider the panel patient, but only on condition that he will queue up at the hour appointed not by the patient, but by the doctor; and that in queueing up he will absolutely divest himself of any vestige of the proper attitude of the customer towards the supplier of service.

In this process of analysing the great public mind we find that underlying all the assumptions is the last that I will mention, the assumption that all men are alike; an assumption that is carried to its logical conclusion by a logical, bureaucratic Moscow; an assumption that is simply devastating in its reactions.

That, it will be said, is an exaggerated picture. But it should be remembered that it does not, of course, mean that all government is bad—that we

can do without government. It does mean, however, that government is too serious, too responsible,
too risky an undertaking to enter upon lightly, and
that no extension of the powers or functions of
government should be permitted until it is demonstrated beyond any possibility of doubt that there is
no other way of achieving the desired end. Such
agitations as are now proceeding in connection with
the Ministry of Transport or the Food Council
ought, in my judgment, to be suspended, as they require far more consideration than is possible in the
circumstances before any of the proposals they put
forward can be justified.

Hooker told us that no prince or potentate ought
to propound a law except by " express commission
immediately and personally received from God,"
or by the consent of the persons upon whom it was
proposed to impose the law. " Laws they are not,"
says Hooker, " which public approbation hath not
made so." I am not informed whether the Ministry
of Transport has received express commission immediately and personally from God, but I submit
that nothing in the nature of public approbation can
be claimed for the latest of its products, the Road
Traffic Bill, with its ninety-two clauses.

A simple illustration of the bill's effect, if it become law, can be found in Clause 62. Under the
bill, the taxi-driver who may think that his carburet-
tor is not working satisfactorily and may wish to
substitute one of another make, will have his attention called by an official to this clause, which says :
" That on any alteration being made in the structure

or equipment of the vehicle he must forthwith give notice to the Public Services Vehicles Examiner of the licensing authority which granted the license, and if he fails to do so shall be guilty of an offence.''

Ninety-two such clauses!—which mean in plain English the arresting of any progress in the matter of transport in this country, and the setting up of yet another oppressive bureaucracy.

Or take the present agitation to re-establish the Ministry of Food. We are the best fed nation in the world because our food has hitherto been left to the free play of individual enterprise, spurred and checked and perfected by competition. In the course of a few months, we have lost the advantages of cream; fish, fruit and other delicacies are becoming scarcer, and the next generation is likely to be better supplied with forms and to be correspondingly short of nourishment.

There is an even more serious side to this tendency in the State mind to override the individual, a side on which there is not even a shadow of a joke, and that is the danger which it presents to the democratic system itself. We are the guardians of the sacred trust of democracy, and to-day we are abusing that trust in such a way that when, as must happen presently, our 30,000,000 electors discover that food and houses are not made with votes, they will give up the votes and abandon the blessings of the democratic system.

The assumption is that 30,000,000 people in the exercise of the franchise can manage everything. They cannot. The assumption is that they can know everything. They cannot. These are assumptions full of danger, to which it is necessary to call serious public attention if we are to get back to a recognition of the position of the individual, for it is obvious that one of the rights of the individual is to know about his particular job rather better than others, and certainly better than the Government.

We are such poor guardians of the democratic institutions secured for us at the cost of immense effort and sacrifice by our forefathers that the chief use we make of the power to govern ourselves is, day by day, to pass larger and larger slices of that power over to an ever-increasing and ever more oppressive bureaucracy.

If the matter were not so serious there would be a funny side to it. Think of society as a crowd standing on the pavement of Fleet Street looking at the Lord Mayor's Show. One bright individual hits upon the idea of getting a soap box and standing on it. Thus he can see better than the rest of the crowd. That is a good and sensible notion from his point of view. But presently everybody gets a soap box—and each box is labelled " work or maintenance," " right to live," " insurance," " grant in aid," " subsidy," " safeguard," " tariff," " dole," " pension," or " guarantee "; and the only result is that the whole crowd of which society is composed, instead of standing upon the firm foundation of Mother Earth, is balancing upon a flimsy basis of soap boxes which must in time collapse.

We have poured out the national income to carry out what I may call the soap box policy until we have arrived at an expenditure of £3 per week per family—that being the sum that week by week goes into and comes out of the public purse.

What, then, is the remedy? How can we restore purity to democratic government and free the individual from bureaucratic oppression? I believe that it is time to think matters over again, to examine carefully the policy of Individualism, the policy which once put Britain and the British in a position rather higher than that of any other country or any other people. Our Individualist case is strengthened when we reflect that these modern tendencies are built upon bad history, for the time has yet to come when we shall have a really reliable popular history of the Industrial Revolution and of the Victorian period. Such a history will have to be written in a new tone and a new light, so that we may begin to realise some of the blessings that were given to us in those glorious days.

Reference has already been made to the disquieting fact that this country has now to accept a second position from the point of view of the subsistence of the people. The United States of America is a stronghold of Individualism, in the economic sphere; and America has produced a standard of living far ahead of anything that we have attained here. That difference needs to be brought out by inviting a broad comparison of Britain and America.

The prevailing opinion in the United States may

be said to move in the opposite direction to prevailing opinion in this country.

Imagine those two old gentlemen, John Bull and Uncle Sam, each explaining his point of view to his worker son. What they are saying to-day is, I think, something like this :

JOHN BULL : You are a good fellow, do the best you can; don't kill yourself at it. You were not made for work; a happy life is what you came here for. If you find things too hard for you, there is an insurance fund and a dole and an old-age pension at your service. If at all times our arrangements for your well-being and comfort do not in every way meet with your approval, you can rely on the Government, or the universities, or the trade unions, or some other highly intellectual body of persons to devise new means for your perfect comfort.

So much for John Bull. What is Uncle Sam's advice?

UNCLE SAM : You are a man : you are as good as any other man; anything which any other man can do you can do if you will try. Life is not a bed of roses; it is a struggle with the forces of Nature. The world depends upon work, effort and endeavour on your part, and on the part of everybody else. If you succeed you help to lift others up; if you fail you help to push others down. So get out and get on, and be quick about it; and, above all, remember that you are an American citizen and that America is destined to lead mankind.

It surely cannot be denied that the whole force of

public opinion in this country is directed to teaching our people to lean, whereas on the other side of the Atlantic the whole force of public opinion is directed to encouraging the people to push. That is, in a single sentence, the difference between the Individualist and the Collectivist conceptions of the State, and from our point of view it is a very dangerous difference.

We plead for a return to the Individualist point of view. We should concentrate our thoughts on men and women as individuals, realising that each one of them represents a piece of God's best work, and that the task before us is to give them a chance to do their own best work in their own way.

CHAPTER III

DISCONTENT is the mainspring of action, and if applied to constructive purposes, it is to be encouraged.

A certain amount of Socialism is good for any nation. It provides a background of criticism and comment which keeps the work of the nation constantly under examination and forms a safeguard against complacency and satisfaction, dangers that would bring any society to an end; but in these days, ten years after the war, we have a rather larger proportion of Socialism than is good or convenient.

The reason is not hard to seek. The useful Socialist, the man who helps society, is always under 30 years of age. The dangerous Socialist, and there are never very many of them, is the man of over 50. It is the men and women of from 30 to 50 who do the work of the nation and on whom the criticism of the young Socialist and the cynicism of the old Tories act as useful spurs and brakes. At 30 the normal man and woman begin to realise that happiness and prosperity depend upon their personal efforts, and 30 is the age when the active Individualist starts on all the things that really matter to society.

Thus we see why, at the moment, we are overdone with Socialism. We are some millions short of men of 30. The war did that for us. Another ten years will put the matter right, but for the moment we are paying what is, perhaps, the heaviest

34

item in the war bill, suffering from the lack of a generation of manhood which could and would, were it here, make England a much better place. The gospel of Individualism has been forgotten except by the few.

There is, however, as always happens in human affairs, a certain amount of compensation or balance, and Socialism itself is wearing out. No story, however silly, will last for ever, and for years and years nothing has been added to or altered in the silly Socialist story. It was told as it had never been told before, and is never likely to be told again, by Robert Blatchford in 1894, when he published that jolly book appropriately called "Merrie England." A study of Blatchford's exposition of Socialism brings out very clearly the fact that not a syllable, not a thought, not a notion worth the name has been added to Socialism since Blatchford wrote.

He said it all thirty-four years ago, and, as one would expect from so charming a fellow as Nunquam of the *Clarion*, he has by this time almost given it up. But "Merrie England" remains the best of all the Socialist writings. It is, as I have said, a jolly book; it bubbles with a sense of humour; it is enlivened with funny little drawings of Capitalistic monkeys, and it sends you to bed after an evening's reading without a headache and with a sense of satisfaction.

I turn to Blatchford for relief after my daily study of the stodgy nonsense so continuously poured out as the current literature of Socialism. Its authors are all so dolefully serious, so ignorantly earnest, and so conceitedly cocksure.

Blatchford, the reader may remember, adopts the Ruskin trick, but instead of addressing a working man, directs his remarks to Mr. John Smith, " a staunch Liberal " and " a shrewd, hard-headed, practical man," whom he appropriately locates at Oldham. " How," asks Blatchford, " are we to make the best of our country and of our lives? " I like the introduction of " our country," a note which modern Socialists have lost. " What things," he goes on, " do we need in order to secure a happy, healthy, and worthy human life? We may divide the things needful into two kinds—mental and physical. That is to say, the things needful for the body and the things needful for the mind."

" The bodily needs are two—health and sustenance. The mental needs are three—knowledge, pleasure and intercourse." " As to sustenance, there are four chief things needed to sustain life in a civilised community—food, clothing, shelter, and fuel " : and from this simple and entirely human and practical starting-point Blatchford runs off his delightful story of the Socialist State.

We need not bother with the story in detail. To begin with, he takes us back to the land and feeds us from the produce of our own little island, which is enough to show that " Merrie England " must be classified as fiction and is devoid of serious economics. The book is crammed full of the bad arithmetic and bad logic which are the common currency of Socialism. That one would expect, but it is not often, even in far worse Socialist writings, that one finds such complete self-exposure as Blatchford gives us.

His enthusiasm for the cause which he was then preaching led him into the unfortunate indiscretion of printing in two lines cheek by jowl the two following sentences. He is speaking of the workers, and he tells us that " they would receive all the produce of their labour." The very next sentence reads, " Pensions would be granted to the ancient poor." It never occurs to Blatchford that if everyone receives all the produce of his labour, there is no produce left wherewith to pay pensions or any other public or social service. Some Socialists overcome this sort of difficulty by a boastful denial of logic as if it were an antiquated and unnecessary capitalistic device. Blatchford is genuinely and happily ignorant of anything so horridly practical. But even this sort of thing does not spoil one's affection for Robert Blatchford. He was the perfectly charming young man Socialist of thirty years ago, and it is just as well that the young man, whether Socialist or not, should be free from the restraint which comes with middle age and experience.

When he wrote " Merrie England," however, Blatchford was getting very near to the age of discretion, while still retaining some of his youthful *naïveté*. " These are my ideas," he says. " They are very crude, and, of course, very imperfect. But don't trouble on that score. When your public understands Socialism and desires to establish it there will be no difficulty about plans. Just get a number of your cleverest organisers and administrators into committee and let them formulate a scheme."

Seeing that in the meantime we have had Dr. Addison and committees by the million, I think I am justified in claiming that Socialism is worn out. But Blatchford appeals to me in quite another way. He talks of " Merrie England," and he tacks on his Socialism to a lovable form of Nationalism which is quite irresistible. Listen to this :

" Now, then, what is the problem? I call it the problem of life. We have here a country and a people. The problem is—given a country and a people, find how the people may make the best of the country and of themselves. First, then, as to the capacities of the country and the people. The country is fertile and fruitful, and well stored with nearly all the things that people need. The people are intelligent, industrious, strong and famous for their perseverance, their inventiveness and resource. It looks, then, as if such a people in such a country must certainly succeed in securing health and happiness and plenty for all."

Since the war it has been fashionable to talk of world problems, and every little parish councillor thinks, and thinks justly, that he has some share of responsibility for putting the world right. I propose to tackle the world through the individuals of whom it is composed, and not, as too many of the parish councillors would have us do, through world-wide arrangements in which scarcely anyone be-lieves and which would never work to whatever extent belief were imposed in them.

Building a perfect world is not unlike any other building job, and must start with the foundations. However perfect a roof is constructed at Geneva or elsewhere it will tumble to pieces unless it rests upon a decent, honest, clean and healthy individual down below. I can, therefore, claim to be concerned with the well-being of the world while disclaiming any interest in the modern habit of world arrangements. My way and the politicians' way have nominally the same aim in view, but my way will get there.

I would not therefore talk about the world, but about England. We can tackle England and we can make it a better place. That is a comparatively simple little job which is within our own powers and capabilities, but if we were to succeed in making England a perfect place we could not fail to make the world a better place, for the world would copy England. It has always done so.

I have no sympathy with patriotism or nationalism of the Jingo kind, but patriotism is like that economic entity competition, and is capable of much misunderstanding. There is good patriotism and there is bad patriotism, just as there is good competition and bad competition. Either of these things, if founded upon a desire to be better oneself, is thoroughly good, healthy and desirable. Either of them, if founded upon a mere desire to beat the other fellow, is bad, unhealthy and undesirable.

Build up the argument in this way. If we had a perfect world it would include a perfect England.

A perfect England involves a perfect you and me, and I therefore propose, as Blatchford would say, that you and I, Mr. Smith, take a rest now and again from going to Westminster to put each other right, and that we spend a little time at home in the endeavour each to get himself right. If that endeavour succeeded, then we should be a good deal nearer to a right England, if indeed we did not find that the task was accomplished. And a right England would be a good big step towards a right world.

It is not necessary to be a Jingo or to be conceited to believe that England, this tiny little island, Merrie England as it might be called, has in point of fact given to the world everything that it possesses except art, music and philosophy.

Nobody will deny that England has set a standard for the world in the matter of government. England produced the mother of all Parliaments, England has developed the democratic system, and in these respects England has a responsibility to the world as a whole. If, having discovered and perfected these undoubted blessings, we now abuse them, on our heads will rest the blame if the rest of the world also makes havoc of democracy and government. If by insisting that the democratic principle shall build houses and dig coal we fail, as, of course, we shall fail, we shall bring the democratic principle into disrepute, and the world will fast lose it. Democracy, therefore, is entitled to look to England to save and preserve her own child from utter and complete destruction.

No sane person, however unpatriotic or however class conscious he or she may be, will deny that England gave to the world the arts of manufacture and the science of trade. Neither will any responsible student deny that these things were developed in England by individual enterprise, and that our modern policy threatens to throw away its manufactures and its trade and to substitute industrial stagnation and the inactivity of Collectivism.

So I go back to Blatchford, and I ask for Merrie England. I call on the Englishman to assert himself, not in any spirit of boastfulness, but in that sporting way that the English, of all people, really understand.

Let us believe, as we are entitled to believe, that the Englishman is the best thing civilization has yet produced, and that we can, if we will, as an English race, develop a standard and a life which shall not only be happy and comfortable for ourselves, but which will be available by example to the rest of the world. Other nations are, of course, quite entitled to think better of themselves than they do of us, and if through competition and patriotism they are able to do better than we, they will in their turn render us the service of an example which we could with a clear conscience copy. Let us have, in a word, competition and patriotism for good.

The Merrie England of the future will differ from the Merrie England of the past. There will be nothing feudal about it. It will be entirely free from social snobbery. We are almost rid of the snobbery of what used to be regarded as the governing classes. Our dukes and lords and millionaires are among the most humble people in the land, but we must resist the growth of the new snobbery. Our modern governors the bureaucrats, whether they draw their salaries from rates and taxes or from trade union funds, are in a fair way to establish a new brand of snobbishness, a new class consciousness, which is far worse than anything which oppressed us in feudal times.

Class consciousness is preached by people imbued with social snobbery and anxious to reap its rewards. Social snobbery is rapidly dying in the ranks of peers and baronets and bishops and other functionaries, who have after all some historic claim to be snobs, but it is developing fast and furious in other classes of life.

The trade union official is often a frightful snob. Your big trade union snob will talk eloquently about the workers and call them comrades from the platform, but the comradeship in question does not, with some of them at least, extend to the length of a game of bowls on a Sunday afternoon. Merrie England must rid itself of snobbery, and surely the real Englishman can be, if he will, as free from this particular vice as any living creature.

By way of balance, for all things in life require to be balanced, we may have to develop, or rather re-develop, the patriotism of the Englishman, that delightful sense of national pride to which no human being is more entitled than the solid, sure, phlegmatic, typical English philosopher. He must come out of his shell and begin to assert himself again.

He has overdone the self-effacement line of con-
duct, he just goes on quietly with the job, irritated
if he gets any credit for it and lets the other man
point out his failings, while he smokes his pipe or
digs his garden or plays his game of golf.

The world wants more talk from the Englishman.
There is no fear of his ever becoming spoilt with
success like, for instance, the American. One of
the few things that make me sometimes doubt the
wisdom of material prosperity is the way in which
it has puffed up the American. If slums and
poverty and unemployment are essential to keep us
humble, then perhaps there may be something to
be said for these evils, but the Merrie Englishman
will always be humble and need not have his slums
and his poverty. We can always learn from others,
but we must not forget that we have also something
to teach.

CHAPTER IV

PRODUCTION VERSUS POVERTY

THIS will be known as the Age of the Committee, when activity was reduced to its minimum by the simple and popular device of passing all responsibility over to somebody else. Many well-intentioned but deluded persons—even persons to whom is not attached the Socialist label—conceive that the well-being of forty-three million individuals can be "organised." My ideas are not so wildly ambitious. I give the Almighty credit for having put into the brains of most of these millions rather more sense and ability than any politician is willing to admit; and instead of organising them I only want to encourage each and every one of them to develop his native talents. This is because I believe in the Gospel of Individualism and realise its tremendous import to the people of this country.

The wealth of nations consists of Things. Poverty is the absence of a sufficient number of things. It is not a mere question of bread or houses, but of how much bread and how many houses in relation to the number of people. We need more arithmetic and less cackle in the consideration of these matters.

Let us try to discover what it is that people want and how far it is possible to supply those wants. We shall be helped in our quest if we go back a little and, by way of preparation, try to find out and put down what people wanted, say, one hundred years ago; what they had then and how far their wants have been met; what we now have, and examine the machinery and the processes that have brought about the improvement—if improvement there has been; see how, with our present knowledge, such machinery can be bettered and, generally discarding theory and rhetoric, do a little practical business study in arithmetic.

First of all, where did people live a hundred years ago? There were ten or twelve millions of them in these little islands at the beginning of last century. Where did they sleep? What did they eat? What did they do when it rained? How did they keep themselves warm?

There is plenty of evidence to show that a very limited number of aristocrats and a comparatively limited number of middle-class people lived in fair comfort. They never bathed, managed without soap, and their behaviour was like that of savages in comparison with most of our modern habits. But they were able to enjoy life.

I have, however, been quite unable to discover (and I have searched long and earnestly) where and how nine-tenths of the British citizens of this time lived. My own belief is that the conditions which now prevail in places like the South of Ireland and the interior of Brittany were common here, and that our ancestors dragged out an existence in turf hovels or mud huts—and other habitations to match—and that most of them were far nearer in their material condition to Adam than they were to us.

It is beyond dispute that three-fourths of all the

houses that now stand in this country have been built since 1850. It is equally beyond dispute that the vast majority of all the dwellings in which we now find shelter were built in the last few years of last century, when private enterprise and speculation were encouraged in the building trade.

What did our ancestors of a hundred years ago wear? Were there such things as underclothes as we know them? Or is it a fact that a garment, once laboriously made by hand, was passed from father to child until, when it failed to hang together, bits of it were patched into some other garment for the next generation.

We know that in 1850 the total consumption of wool in the United Kingdom was 18lb. per head of the population per annum. We know that 500,000 bales of cotton had to do the work now done by 3,500,000 bales. And all the available statistics show that 100 years ago the material resources of mankind were a mere fraction of those at our service to-day.

What did our ancestors eat? A hundred years ago the consumption of sugar amounted to 3oz. per week per head. To-day every man, woman and child among us consumes in some form or another 3lb. of sugar every week of his or her life.

Meat as a regular element in diet was almost unknown, until Individualism produced the Industrial Revolution and the abolition of poverty thus became for the first time a practical proposition.

Or tackle the same problem the other way round,

and look at our standards to-day to see how they fit the past. The enormous disparity is clearly seen if we jot down the doings of the normal modern man in a normal day and consider their relation to the industrial developments of the last century or two. A bank clerk may be regarded as a good average specimen of the majority of us as we live in the year 1928. His life may be taken as typical of the life of most people who work for a living. Here is an abbreviated sketch of a day in the life of such an individual.

On waking he finds his head on a feather pillow. He is covered with a cotton sheet spread over a wool or hair mattress, supported by springs. He steps out of bed on to a piece of carpet, looks at his watch, takes a cup of hot water or hot tea, which was prepared with the heat from a gas stove. He washes himself with soap and a sponge, brushes his teeth, puts his clothes on in a matter of five minutes, thanks to bone and metal buttons, and goes down to breakfast.

He drinks coffee, tea, cocoa, as he fancies, sweetened with sugar, swallows a mouthful of marmalade, dropping some of it on the tablecloth. He puts on a mackintosh, and, armed with an umbrella in one hand and gloves in the other, sets out for the City. On the way he buys a newspaper, tobacco and matches. He makes the journey in a train, tram, or omnibus, on a road paved and drained, and then he begins to do a day's work that in almost every detail was not thought of 200 years ago.

On returning home at night he has a currant bun or a piece of chocolate cake with his tea, and a supper of frozen meat, after which he sits on a little grass lawn, or perhaps tends his roses. He will then change his boots and read a novel or play a game of bridge. Before retiring for the night he will, perhaps, write a letter to a friend to arrange a cycle ride for the following Sunday, and then proceed to take off his clothes and get into a nightshirt or pyjamas. He will open his bedroom window, turn off the gas or electric light and try to forget everything till the following morning.

A careful study of this simple story will disclose the fact that there is scarcely a thought or action or thing in the whole of it that would have passed through the mind or been done or existed 200 years ago. To begin with, of course, bank clerks, in any numbers, were not wanted 200 years ago. Trade has not only produced the bank clerk himself, but it has produced everything that he does and touches, and all that goes to make up life for him, from which it follows that without trade life itself would be impossible.

This is not the place to enter upon a dissertation concerning the highly technical question of population, but it may be noted in passing that while population remained more or less stationary for thousands of years, it only began to grow when modern trade began to function, so that we may say, as we read or write these lines, that we might not have been here to do either were it not for trade.

All the little comforts and conveniences, such as they are, which help to make the life of the bank clerk tolerable, might by now have been equally available to every working man and woman. Indeed all might have had much more. We know from the experience of America how rapidly wealth is spread where trade is left free to function. Seeing indeed that we had a good long start of America, wealth should be more general here than there. But as we have allowed the politicians and the Collectivists to impose their theories upon our business classes and to squander our wealth on artificial restraints and hindrances, most of us are still comparatively poor.

And now we can get straight down to our arithmetic. Suppose we set the problem like this : Let us give to some railway porter of our acquaintance another £5 a week. Let us make an arrangement whereby this worthy fellow, with his life mapped out on a basis of 45s., is assured of an income of £7 5s. What would he do? What changes would he make? What exactly would happen? I think there are probably nine simple things, among a great many others, that would happen right away.

1. He would move into a better house, with a bath room.
2. He would get himself another suit of clothes.
3. He would buy himself another pair of boots, so that he could change from day to day and give the wet ones a chance to dry before he put them on again.
4. He would buy a new hat for himself, and if his wife were a frugal woman, a couple of hats for her.
5. He would double his consumption of coal, and enjoy a

4

fire when he now frequently goes without, and he would bring his coal account up to, say, two tons a year for each member of his family.

6.   For the first time in his life he would give himself the luxury of an umbrella.

7.   He might buy a mackintosh.

8.   If he had a daughter he would probably acquire a piano on the hire-purchase plan.

9.   He would take a definite step up in society by treating himself to the luxury of a clean collar a day.

These are homely, simple things that don't find a place in political speeches.   It is easy to perorate about £1 a week but not so easy to make speeches about umbrellas or hats.

I have taken the case of a railway porter, and regarded him as if he were a solitary individual with an additional £5 a week.   But it is quite impossible to found any public policy, or any political programme or any scheme of social reform upon the circumstances of one individual, or even upon those of a single class of individuals.   National wealth is concerned with the wealth of us all.

If we now give to our hypothesis a wider, more sensible basis, and picture what would happen if £5 a week were added to the wealth, or to the power of material enjoyment of all of us, we begin to see the real nature of the difficulties so freely discussed to-day and so little understood.   Let us suppose, for the sake of this argument, that the adult male portion of the nation is composed of railway porters whose income it is proposed to increase by £5 a week each.

Our supposition gives rise to an easy problem

in arithmetic—43,000,000 people divided into 10,000,000 families, the head of each family, like our railway porter, to have £5 per week added to his income. We will assume, again only for the sake of simplicity, that each of them will use the £5 a week in the way that we have suggested the money would be employed by the single railway porter whom we took as our original example. Dealing with the points in the order in which we placed them before :

1. The first thing we require is 10,000,000 decent houses. There exist at the moment certainly not more than 2,000,000 houses which would satisfy railway porters having an income of £7 5s. a week, so that on the instant we need 8,000,000 homes, or, stated in different terms, as many as the united efforts of the Government and the municipalities and private owners could build at the present rate in the next forty years. No amount of money will achieve this object. The trouble arises from the absence of bricks and timber, and all the material things that go to make up a house, and, chiefly, from the absence of the most important of all—individual effort. It is a sad reflection when we remember that thirty years ago private enterprise and competition had discovered the way to fill this need and was just about to accomplish the task, when political interference stopped all building progress and halved the personnel of the building industries.

The 200,000 houses a year from which the Ministry of Health and all its satellites derive such satisfaction are barely sufficient to replace worn-out houses. If 10,000,000 homes is the proper figure for our population, and if we give to every home a life of fifty years, it will be seen that 200,000 houses a year are necessary to replace those that wear out. A very small proportion of all the houses built can hope to survive the slum test fifty years after their erection.

We further gave to our railway porter a house with a bathroom, which means in our bigger sum that we should have in this country to-day 10,000,000 baths, with an equal number of hot-water systems, and of all the paraphernalia that go to make up a normal bathroom.

2. We next imagine that our railway porter would get himself another suit of clothes. If we allow—and it is surely not unreasonable—that a man with £7 5s. a week would expect to have himself, and to give to his wife and to his children three suits or dresses per annum, then the market for clothes in this country alone is represented by 135,000,000 outfits a year—a quantity well beyond the most optimistic dreams of the most enterprising Selfridge.

3. To provide each of us with two pairs of boots a year, which was suggested as a third item in the railway porter's programme, will increase the home demand on the boot market to 90,000,000 pairs.

4. If, like the railway porter, each of the men had a hat a year, while each woman had three, we get an immediate demand for more than 60,000,000 hats—a figure, I presume, that has never been approached by any hat trade outside America.

5.   If every working-class family were able, as is here suggested, to double its consumption of coal, the grave problems of that industry would quickly disappear.

6.   A simple little item like an umbrella, if we give to it a life of a couple of years and restrict its use to the adult population, means a trade of 15,000,000 umbrellas per annum.

7.   Similarly, with mackintoshes. Supposing we argue that a child does not want a mackintosh until it reaches school age, and that here again we give to the average mackintosh a life of two years, we find that our requirements amount to about 20,000,000 mackintoshes a year.

8.   There are, so far as I can ascertain, about 1,000,000 pianos in our homes at the present time. To put our railway porter right we require, therefore, at once, 9,000,000 more.

9.   If it were possible, as we have suggested, for every man in the country to have a clean collar every day of his life, the laundry trade would be called upon to handle more than 5,000,000,000 collars a year. The soap trade, with all its wonderful capacity, would be inadequate to the demand.

Furthermore, if we allow to each man no more than one dozen new collars a year—a meagre allowance unless laundry science is greatly improved— we find that our requirements are no less than 180,000,000 collars, with all that that means to the cotton and linen industries.

If I am right in thinking that most of the votes given to the Socialists are given by people who have visions of an additional £5 a week, then do we revert to this list of things that are wanted, and, mark, wanted now :

8,000,000	houses.
135,000,000	clothing outfits.
90,000,000	pairs of boots.
60,000,000	hats.
15,000,000	umbrellas.
20,000,000	mackintoshes.
9,000,000	pianos.
180,000,000	collars.

All these things and much besides would quickly appear on a free market in which we were all at liberty to exercise our capabilities to the full. There is however no hope of any such development of wealth so long as we are afflicted with all our present Collectivist restraints on individual activity. The job is too big to organise, but split up into forty million little jobs is easily within our compass.

But these facts emphasise the truth of the theory that the problem of poverty is not a problem of money, but of things, and that if we will make the things the problem disappears. Things are made by individuals. How suicidal then are all the multifarious restrictions with which we hedge ourselves around.

Most of the difficulties in the economic world would rapidly be solved if people could be brought to accept and act upon the indubitably true proposition that every piece of work or trade completed leads directly and immediately to another piece of work or trade.

Production comes before consumption and leads to it.   The presence of a supply creates a demand. There is only one exception of which I am aware to this unalterable rule.   No increase in the production of coffins is likely, so far as I can see, to improve the demand upon the coffin trade, but with that single exception I know of no other commodity which would not be more freely consumed if production were increased or accelerated, and thus cheapened.

CHAPTER V

DELAYS AND RESTRICTIONS

BUSINESS men whose experience goes back into the last century will remember a phrase which formed part of almost every business arrangement, and which read: " Time is the essence of the contract." The phrase has fallen out of common use, and in its place there now appears quite a number of elaborate sentences and safeguards setting out the circumstances that may delay the delivery of the goods or the completion of the contract and providing that the supplier is immune from damages on that account.

Strikes, lock-outs, fires, wars, riots, civil commotions, the act of God, and, literally, "all circumstances beyond the control of the contractor," are printed large over estimate forms and business stationery, and, in entering upon a contract of any kind, both parties quite understand beforehand that very wide margins must be allowed, both in price and in time, to cover all the other extraneous considerations which theorists and politicians have in the last twenty-five years imposed upon the old-fashioned simplicity of business.

If for any reason the time occupied to complete a piece of business is extended, expense and loss are incurred, not only on that piece of business, but by all parties associated with it, in respect of the next piece of business that they would normally undertake. If we consider only the question of capital, the damage of delay becomes very evident. It is obviously to the advantage of the worker, the employer, the consumer and every party to a business transaction, that as little capital as possible should be used to carry it through and further that the capital should be used for as short a time as possible.

Even Communists can agree about that. It does not matter to whom the capital belongs, or where it comes from, it is obvious that there must at any time be a limit to the amount of capital available for particular purposes, and that there must also be expense involved in the use of that capital: so that economy in employment of capital or the time involved must bring advantage to all parties.

Consider the case of a builder with a capital of £500. If the cost of a cottage is £500, the builder's capital is just sufficient to put up one cottage. If a cottage takes six months to build the capacity of this particular builder is two cottages a year. If a cottage takes four months to build, the capacity of the builder is three cottages a year. In the first case, each cottage involved the exclusive use of £500 of capital for six months, and in the second case the same amount of capital for four months only. So that, in restriction of output by labour, in delay to output by official regulation or inspection, in the holding up of the building for any reason whatever, there is also involved a restriction of output by capital.

It will be obvious in the simple case of this little builder that, having expended £500, completed his cottage and passed it over to the purchaser or the local authority or the occupier or whoever ordered it, he must immediately proceed to reinvest the £500 in another cottage or in another piece of building of the same value. This is what happens in the normal process of trade. The moment that a merchant or a tradesman sells anything a new purchase is at once made. If the sale is delayed the purchase is likewise delayed. The old theory of small profits and quick returns is still true.

Consider another elementary case from common experience, this time showing how the delay in a piece of work destroys other work. A few years ago the Sunday morning delivery of letters by the Post Office was discontinued. There are many grounds on which it is wise and desirable to do without the Sunday post, and it may well be that on the whole the reasons in favour of the six-day post outweigh the reasons against it. That does not, however, vitiate our economic argument. The abolition of the Sunday post, however good it may be for other reasons, leads directly to unemployment and loss of trade. First of all, there are large numbers of persons who write to one another every day when there is a post. It would not surprise me to know that there are a million such persons. Mothers with daughters at school and sweethearts between them may well account for a million daily letters.

If that be so, there have been six million such letters a week instead of seven million since the Sunday post was abolished. The railways have a million fewer letters to carry; stationers have a million sheets of paper and a million envelopes fewer to handle; paper makers and gum makers suffer; and all these persons in their turn are forced to stop the trade in which they had previously expended the money they received for the materials and services associated with these million discontinued letters.

Mothers and sweethearts, however, are the most elementary part of the story. When the Sunday post was working, the London stores would receive a consignment of goods on a Friday, include them in their catalogues, publish and post on Saturday. The customers would settle their requirements on Sunday; the orders would be back at the stores on Monday, and clerks, packers, carters, railwaymen, to say nothing of packing-case makers, string manufacturers, brown paper mills and hundreds of other suppliers of sundries would be busy on Monday working to complete their orders.

Now, in the absence of the Sunday post, a catalogue is received by the customer on the Monday, the orders reach the store on the Tuesday, and all the many people associated with the execution of the order are out of work on the Monday. It is true that by various rearrangements, by the spreading over of work, by the general acquiescence in delay now common among us, the clerks at the stores do not appear to be out of work on a Monday, but the most perfunctory examination of the case must bring us to the conclusion that the day lost by the absence of the Sunday post is one of the causes of the unemployment about which we are all so deeply concerned.

I am not asking for the reintroduction of the
Sunday post.   My personal convenience may have
some influence on my views in this connection, for
I receive quite enough correspondence on six morn-
ings in the week to make me welcome the Sunday
gap.   There can be no question as to the advantage
to Post Office workers of one day's rest in seven,
and I am not inclined to disagree with those who
think that the whole community is better for a full
twenty-four hours' relief from the activities of the
Post Office.   That is not my point.   I want it to
be understood that the relief from these activities
costs more than appears upon the surface and involves relief also from all the other activities that
would follow from the work and trade involved in
the Sunday post.

Exactly the same sort of thing happens when a
German camera is unloaded and put into the
Custom house at the London docks.   When that
camera is delivered to the purchaser in England the
£5 note, or whatever its value may be, goes at once
to Germany and is used at once by the Germans to
buy Lancashire cotton goods or some other commodity.   I leave out of account all complications.
It is true, of course, that the German may use the
£5 note to buy French champagne, that the French-
man may send it to Turkey for figs, and that the
Turk may be the medium through which it comes to
Lancashire for cotton goods.   If the camera is de-
tained by the Custom officials in the London docks
for a week, or a day, or even an hour, the capital
represented by the camera is kept employed in con-

nection with that particular camera for another week or a day or an hour and is prevented from proceeding with its next mission, the purchase of champagne or figs, and eventually Lancashire cotton goods.

It is easy to pile up illustrations in support of this very simple argument. Consider a piece of paper destined to form part of a book. When this piece of paper is once made quite a number of other transactions become possible in both directions. Any delay in making the piece of paper causes double delay in all those other transactions.

The paper worker, who gets his money for the paper, proceeds at once to spend it on socks and cigarettes or perambulators, spreading employment all around him. The mill-owner, so soon as the piece of paper is made and delivered, gets his capital back and proceeds at once to start his machinery on the making of more paper. The printer to whom the paper goes is thus enabled to make a book. The author who has written the book can get his money for it and can set off on a much-needed holiday, thus employing railwaymen, hotel-keepers, cinema attendants at the seaside, and so on. All these processes in all directions are quite certainly delayed if there is any delay in the production of the original piece of paper, and many of them are rendered impossible if there is any extravagance or waste in connection with the making of the paper.

There is another sort of delay that is very common amongst us—the delay imposed by trade union rule and regulation. The theory is that if two men can be forced into a job instead of one, or if one man can be forced to spread a single day's work over two days, then more wages are secured to the members of the trade unions. This is, of course, a wholly false idea, and its wide-spread acceptance does little credit to our economic intelligence.

If two men are standing on the pavement waiting for a day's work and only one job offers, it does seem natural that the two men should join forces in a union and say they will do the job together and thus help one another, but that is not the real situation. It is the veriest surface of the truth. By joining together and insisting that two men must do the work of one, the trade unions close up the market, and work that would otherwise be required is murdered at its source. All these restrictive arrangements do, indeed, make things a little better for an ever-diminishing privileged few who can keep inside the union or the ring.

For example, the 17,420 gentlemen who now monopolise the art of plastering are able to demand terms in money, though not in real values, which they might not secure in a free market. These 17,420 plasterers are able to say to the rest of us: "We are ordained to plaster; we will do nothing but plaster; we will plaster just as much as we decide and on the terms that we arrange, and nobody shall plaster but us." It is impossible to blame the plasterers, who are allowed by stupid public opinion to adopt and maintain such an attitude, but it is also impossible to deny that when plasterers, bricklayers, masons, carpenters and all the other tradesmen that go to make up the building industry adopt with success the same attitude, the effect of their arrangements is to limit the building market so seriously as to keep us all in discomfort in the matter of houses, and to keep all the innumerable trades that follow the builder in a state of unemployment.

We are very prone to consider only the circumstances of the moment and the considerations which lie upon the surface of a particular business transaction in which we happen to be engaged. Thus we forget that when a worker declines a shilling and strikes or waits for 1s. 2d., not only is the important work which is the subject of the discussion lost to the consumer and the shilling to the worker, but all the work and trade that follow in both directions the moment that the shilling or the 1s. 2d. change hands are also lost. Exactly the same argument applies when a business man, to the order of a price "ring," declines some piece of business until he can impose the terms of the ring.

This is not an argument against the strike for a proper wage or a hold-up for a proper price. There may well be full justification for either action. I am merely concerned to show that when that strike or that hold-up takes place, very much more is involved in it than the mere question of 2d. an hour or the fixed price for the article.

It is far too generally assumed that the 2d. an hour and the fixed price can only be secured through the method of the strike or the price ring. This I believe to be one of the greatest of our modern misconceptions. In my view, if every worker would accept the first job offered at the best price obtainable, and if every business man would apply the same principle to the purchase and the sale of products, wages and prices in real values would rise much more quickly, but from natural causes. The workers and the price-ring mongers would not only achieve their respective objects much more rapidly, but while doing so they would confer inestimable benefits on all the rest of us as well.

Whichever way we look at it, this proposition that every piece of work leads directly to another cannot, I think, be controverted. The proposition is, however, worthy of the most serious study because of its depth and because of its unending ramifications. The connection between one piece of work and another is so difficult to trace.

The absence of work in the coalfields from May to November, 1926, put the railways in difficulties, closed down the blast furnaces and pottery kilns and made the production of gas expensive. Those simple results, only once removed from the coalfields themselves, are obvious to everybody, but what most people forget is that the railway shareholders and the railway workers, all the people interested in or associated with steel, and the pottery makers of all classes, were all prevented during those seven months from proceeding with the next pieces of work connected with their multifarious requirements. The absence of work in the coal mines led to the stoppage of work in every other trade and industry.

There may be very good reasons for delaying trade and work in various ways.   It is bad for people to overwork; undue pressure is highly undesirable; some work may need inspection by officials or others; there may be good political reasons for excluding work from Russia or the products of slave labour; medical considerations may necessitate the prohibition of some sorts of work or trade.   A hundred considerations may properly apply to this problem, but nothing can alter the economic fact—and this should be more widely and generally understood—that every restraint and every delay, however good and however necessary, does involve the loss of all the business all round which would follow if the delay or restraint were removed.

Every bit of work or trade may be likened to a pebble dropped into a pool, which causes an unending series of ripples.   There may be good reasons why the pebble should not be thrown into the pool, but it should never be forgotten that absence of the pebble involves also the absence of the ripples.

CHAPTER VI
ETHICS AND ECONOMICS

IT is generally very hard, especially in political discussion, to get a clear issue. If cause and effect are not hopelessly confused, the objective is so many-sided as to make simplicity of argument generally very difficult.

Blatchford, although in his "Merrie England" he does not succeed in maintaining the distinction, starts out by dividing very clearly and definitely the things which are needful for the body and those which are good for the mind. He says that "the bodily needs are two—health and sustenance. The mental needs are three—knowledge, pleasure, and intercourse." We shall find ourselves hopelessly entangled in the work of making the world worth while unless we draw a definite, logical, and obvious distinction between the ethical and material.

The Universities do not teach chemistry in the schools of philosophy, or philosophy or divinity as a part of mathematics. It is true, of course, that a chemist is a better man if he is also a philosopher, and that the mathematician will get more enjoyment out of life if he knows something about theology, but to succeed in any of the many departments of thought and action it is essential to concentrate, to specialise and to separate. The muddle of present-day politics is due, perhaps more than to anything else, to the way in which we confuse and try to intermix the ethical and material.

If a man who cannot swim is pushed off the parapet of London Bridge he will drown without any regard whatever to the ethical circumstances associated with the push that caused him to fall. It does not matter whether he was pushed over by his child in play, by his enemy with intent to murder, by the carelessness of a motor-'bus driver, or fell over owing to excess of alcoholic liquor. Ethical problems galore arise from the circumstances that caused him to fall, but eternal study of these ethical problems will not prevent his drowning when once the physical act of falling has commenced.

Or again, my knowledge of chemistry is limited to the fact that carbon dioxide has a way of turning lime-water milky, and lime-water will become milky under the influence of carbon dioxide whether the two things are brought together by a Communist in Moscow, by a Pope in the Vatican or by Mr. Lloyd George and Lord Birkenhead in a coalition cabinet.

No more grotesque or distressing example of the danger of the confusion of ethical ideas and economic laws is, I think, to be found anywhere than in the message which the Archbishop of York, then Bishop of Manchester, addressed to the Copec Conference in Birmingham in 1924. The Bishop dealt with many matters, and amongst them the housing of the working classes. In this connection he said:

" There must be sacrifice of money in the most prosaic and therefore most testing form of increased rates and taxes . . . readily voted and readily paid. Let no one think this unspiritual. It calls for little devotion of spirit to give generously when imagination is fired or feelings are touched; it takes a deeper dedication to lead us gladly to vote for an increase of public expenditure over which our personal control is slight and indirect. It is true that such expenditure is true economy; the money so spent is more than compensated by the human values secured. Where vital human needs are in question we must be ready for financial sacrifice.

"We have seen afresh the meaning of Christ's Passion. He reigns from the Tree."

This passage, typical in every way of much of the nonsense that well-meaning people talk in these times, if closely studied and examined cannot fail to demonstrate the folly of the method. What are the facts? At the end of the nineteenth century this country was overbuilt. Many of the buildings were not of the sort that we should build to-day; many of them were inadequate to house the people who had advanced in education and in social habits far beyond their immediate predecessors, but there were more houses in the country than the people were willing or able to occupy. The population was slowly but surely moving out of old houses into newer ones, and from bad houses into better ones. The building trade had reached dimensions bigger than ever before or ever since, and we possessed the capacity and the facilities for building up to the maximum of our requirements. Building was one of our biggest industries; bricks and mortar were our favourite investment, and almost everybody entertained the ambition of saving a few pounds and owning a house.

Then politicians came upon the scene, and the

notion developed that rates and taxes should be used for building, and the notion spread like wildfire. Land legislation, building Acts and building schemes filled the air.

In course of time a Ministry of Health was developed, and hundreds of millions of public money were spent upon building. In the twenty-five years from 1900 to 1925 we spent more public money upon building houses for the working classes than was spent upon civil Government and all public purposes of every kind, except war, in the whole of the century from 1800 to 1900.

Notice the results. By 1925 the personnel of the building trade, the bricklayers, the masons, the slaters, the plasterers, the carpenters and the rest of them, had dwindled to half the numbers of 1900. The price of houses had multiplied to three or four times the figure of a quarter of a century before. The habit of investing in house property had been almost completely abolished. Nobody now puts a penny into bricks and mortar unless he is obliged to do so in order to find somewhere to live. Public debt had swollen to enormous figures, and our capacity to house ourselves had been reduced to one house per family per century.

It is true that municipalities with much talk and much advertisement have, most of them, cleared some little area on their outskirts and erected a bunch of houses which, in the bulk and on the surface, make it appear as if some building were being done. There can, however, be no dispute that the total of all such building amounts in fact to less than the total of the building that was done by other methods. So it is true to say that rates and taxes had actually robbed us of half the houses we might have had, and yet so completely have we allowed ourselves to be deceived by mixing and muddling ethical considerations with economic laws, that the distinguished Archbishop is able at the end of this melancholy story, with a clear conscience and with public approbation, to claim the authority of the Master whom he serves for " increased rates and taxes " to cause us still further deprivation of houses.

I admit, of course, that my view of the economic side of the housing problem is a matter of opinion. I am not so foolish as to suppose that because I believe in private enterprise in building it is impossible that some day, in some society, some other system may produce houses; but houses are not made of sermons, they consist of bricks and mortar. They do not materialise from philosophy; they are strictly material things.

When a bricklayer lays one brick upon another he provides a small piece of material wealth which will bring comfort and health and happiness to other people, if the brick is well laid, for perhaps a century. Nothing can alter this simple fact, and, as a matter of economics, any consideration of the bricklayer's motive or of the aspirations and ideas which actuated and caused him to lay one brick upon another, is totally irrelevant and immaterial. It does not concern the brick and the need for it and the use of it, whether the bricklayer does it in

order to buy a new frock for his baby or in order to
buy prussic acid to murder his wife. The only
thing that matters on the economic side of the
problem is that the brick should be well and truly
laid in its proper and appropriate place.

Socialists—and even Blatchford must take his
share of blame in this respect—try to make the best
of both worlds and try to have it both ways in this
matter of the ethical and material. They wax eloquent against riches. There is, of course, a very
strong ethical case against the misuse of riches. It
is very important that we should each of us be
taught how to use such riches as we secure, and to
entertain the right ideas in our endeavour to secure
riches. But Socialists do not scruple, when it suits
them, to rail against riches as bad in themselves.

Blatchford is more honest than most of them,
and far more logical. He preaches the simple life.
He objects to the possessions of the rich, and he
offers little more than the merest necessities of life
to the citizens of his Merrie England. But the
appeal of the Socialist case to the people as a whole
is an appeal to their very natural desire to possess
riches themselves. The main plank in the programme of the Socialist party, and to a dangerous
extent of every other political party, consists in the
offer to transfer riches from one class to another.
The aspirant for political honours, certainly if he is
a Socialist, says in fact: " If you object to riches,
vote for me, and I will abolish them; if, on the
other hand, you want riches, also vote for me, and
I will give them to you."

It is perhaps too much to hope for perfect logic in public affairs, but the total absence of anything approaching logic in this very common attitude does no credit to us as a people.

There is altogether too much easy acquiescence in the spurious notion of an ethical side to Socialism. Socialism, indeed, in some quarters, as is illustrated by the attitude of the Bishop of Manchester, is credited with being a sort of religion. I do not doubt that there are many thousands of Socialist dupes who are genuinely under the impression that the political faith of their adoption has an ethical or religious side to it, but surely if ethics and economics are to be connected at all, a much more inspiring religion can be built upon Capitalism than ever came out of the degradation of the Socialist idea.

Socialism, if it is associated with anything at all in the public mind, is linked up with the notion of an easy life, whereas religion and ease have little in common. Apart altogether from the economic truth that life is not, and never can be, easy, there are surely some deeper, truer, more ennobling inspirations to be found in the endeavour, the service, the work, the triumph over difficulties which are inseparable from the struggle for existence so unfortunately termed Capitalism.

The common confusion of ideas in material and in ethical matters leads to all sorts of misconceptions which drag us down. Every ill to which man is heir is commonly attributed, not only by the Socialists, but by many other well-meaning people, to economic causes. Whatever we suffer from lack of education, and the suffering in this respect is surely immense, is quite incapable of remedy through the medium of rates and taxes. We can, with advantage, spend rates and taxes on the right sort of education, but we cannot make rates and taxes take the place of the personal and individual effort that is necessary to grow potatoes or to build houses. If education fails to prepare us for the strenuous personal and individual effort which alone can provide for us and for society, then there is something wrong with education. This muddle over the ethical and the material would cease to worry us if we could get a new conception of the service which is rendered to each and all by the individual effort of each of us.

We are too fond of deciding what is the duty of the other fellow. Political schemes are almost entirely concerned with the duty of the other fellow. It is so obvious to the politically minded that all the others are wrong and must be put right. We vote to " make the foreigner pay " or to tax somebody else, but never to impose obligations or restrictions upon ourselves. But the man who knows what the other fellow should do is often a very useless and inefficient person himself. The gift of the gab is rarely given to those who are proficient in more practical and homely things. I recommend in this connection a very simple and illuminating experiment which any reader can make. Ask a business man and a Socialist to tea for, say, Thursday week. Nineteen times out of twenty the business man will pull out his diary, will tell you either that he cannot come to tea, or that he will catch the 4.20, and that, much as he regrets it, he must leave by the 5.45, because he has an appointment at 6.30 which he must keep.

The Socialist, on the other hand, the gentleman who knows everything about everything, whose mind is so soaked in spurious ethics that he has no doubt as to the duty of everybody else, will thank you for your invitation and tell you that he will let you know to-morrow. If he does remember to ring you up, which is very unlikely, he will explain that he would like to come to tea next Thursday week, although he is not sure whether he promised to sit on some committee which he thinks will meet on Wednesday and may adjourn to Thursday, but will you, he asks, give him a ring in the morning, when perhaps he will be able to let you know.

Finally, when the tea party is ready, he will ring you up to say how sorry he is to have caused you any inconvenience, and "do you really want me to come to tea, or would it not be better if you met me at some conference the week after next, but in any case don't wait for me," and he will perhaps come as soon as he can. If he is a politician, as, of course, most Socialists are, these negotiations will be complicated by the introduction of secretaries; two or three people, as well as yourself and your domestic staff, will be kept busily occupied doing nothing, except exhausting their mental and nervous reserves.

Justice is hard to find. There is very little of it

in human affairs, but surely no injustice was ever so complete or so devastating as that which has associated Socialism with morality and Capitalism with the immoral. What could be more immoral, more disastrous, more devilish in all its implications and results than the limitation of human effort which is inseparable from Socialism? What, indeed, can be more degrading than the notions of control which are the bedrock of Socialism? Capitalism, which consists in the serving of the desires of others, has been perverted by false argument, and Socialism, which consists in subjugating and controlling the desires of others, has been twisted into a worthy ideal.

We must get back to Blatchford, and we must separate the things which are needful for the body from those which are needful for the mind. These needs will react upon one another. Socialism could well become a sort of fanatical religion, which argues that comfort and wealth and material well-being are bad for the soul, and must, therefore, be abolished. On those lines Socialism might well claim to have some relation to ethics, but Socialism or political action of any description can seldom be anything but a destroyer of material well-being.

Nothing has stood in the way of our industrial development and the advance of our material well-being except our mania for politics—our collective obsession, our determination to discuss and to regulate every action before we undertake it. We should, by all the rules of progress, be infinitely better off than any Continental nation. Nevertheless, New York, quite justly and properly, looks upon us as part of hopeless Europe, and Mr. Lloyd George earns a living by writing about us for American newspapers as if we were Poles or Bessarabians.

England found out how to make wealth—not money, but things—years before America started. Fifty years ago the standard of life here, with all its faults and failings, was higher, much higher, than had ever been known in human experience in any age or in any country. Then we became addicted to politics, and since that time have been engaged in throwing away our heritage. From an economic point of view politics are far more destructive than war.

Our triumphs of the Victorian era—that period in which we lifted our own people and other peoples of the world out of the slough of their mediæval despond to a civilised state—were achieved before education became a shibboleth. England founded trade and commerce and provided the basis of modern civilisation with a people who, for the most part, were illiterate. How much better could we do to-day after thirty or forty years of education?

Our education is being chiefly used in the manufacture of new political sophistries. When our people reach the stage at which they are able to visualise the needs of a nation of 43,000,000 people, then—and not till then—shall we get a new spirit, a new idea and new enthusiasms. We shall have revealed to our newly-opened eyes the complete and utter folly of most of the things we are doing to-day.

We shall see how, by political means, we are robbing ourselves of the very things that are offered to us by the politicians.

The problem can be stated in plain, unvarnished terms in a few sentences. We are suffering from a surplus of labour and a shortage of wealth. In these circumstances we all of us devote the major part of our energies to the quest for new ways of limiting, restricting, regulating, and restraining the individual actions of man and the production of wealth, with the natural result that the surplus of labour gets greater and the shortage of wealth gets more acute. If we reverse our policy, dismiss politics from our minds, and all of us dedicate ourselves to activity and the production of wealth, we could arrive, and arrive very quickly, at a condition of affairs in which there was a shortage of labour and a surplus of wealth. The economic condition of the world could be changed completely were we but willing to understand that it is the absence of things which produces poverty. So long as we insist upon making the production of things more and more difficult it is not only useless but stupid to complain of poverty.

CHAPTER VII

THE LIMITATIONS OF MONEY

WITHOUT money civilisation could not exist, and yet it sometimes seems as if the misunderstanding of money will bring civilisation to an end.

The reader will remember that in a previous chapter we took the case of a single railway porter, and we gave him an extra £5 a week. We did not, however, trouble to inquire where the £5 came from. He may have got it from a wealthy aunt who died, or somebody may have been taxed to provide it, or the price of some railway service may have been increased. In any of these cases, some other person has been robbed of the opportunity to make a number of purchases, and that opportunity has been transferred to the railway porter.

The giving to this single man of the single £5 note has not added anything whatever to the wealth of the community as a whole. Political action does a great deal of this sort of work. It takes a bit of wealth from one man and gives it to another. Some £300,000,000 a year for social services alone are transferred in that way at present. There may be some people ready to jump to the conclusion that no change occurs in the wealth of the community as a whole as the result of such a transfer, but it is gravely to be doubted whether the transaction is as innocuous in its effects as, *prima facie*, it might seem to be.

If, for instance, the people who provide the £300,000,000 are in any way discouraged by the process and lessen their productive activities to any extent, however small, the wealth of the nation is reduced to that extent. On the other hand—and this is, perhaps, the more serious consideration—should the people who receive the £300,000,000 be in any way encouraged to slacken their productive efforts, then the wealth of the community is again adversely affected. Whatever opinions, however, may be held regarding this aspect, it cannot be argued that the transfer can increase the amount of wealth which is available for all. Political action, therefore, does not contribute anything towards the provision of the 8,000,000 houses, the 135,000,000 suits, or the many other things that we found to be wanting.

It is worth while to consider what would happen if, by some Socialist device, all incomes were fixed at a level agreed upon as completely satisfactory to the recipients. There is no difficulty about forecasting the sequel. Prices would rise, and we should be faced with all the perplexities of adjusting ourselves to a new price level. We have actually, in the last quarter of a century—the period during which the politician has usurped the place of the business man—doubled our wages. We have done it gradually; first came the bricklayers, then the engineers, afterwards the labourers, and so on. As each part of the process has been completed, as each class has pushed up its price, the others have been at a disadvantage until they could do the same. Thus a state of uncertainty prevails, and we go on fooling about with money and sharing out the same inadequate quantity of goods and things.

The money folly can be seen if we look at America, the land of the almighty dollar. America has little poverty, no absence of things. She has developed mass production and the theory of output to the point when she finds it necessary to flood the world with her surplus. Although prices in America are high, nobody bothers about that. America is obsessed with the twin ideas of production and efficiency, two ideas which have never yet been popular with us, except, perhaps, in connection with such things as newspapers, cigarettes and sweets.

When we accept those ideas we can abolish poverty just as surely as America has done. England is over-politicalised.

Compare England with France or Germany, and compare all three with America. The standard of living, the wealth per head of the population, is in England, France and Germany roughly on a level by comparison with America. America is at least miles ahead of any one of the three of us. In England, we are, perhaps, a little better off than they are in France or Germany, but only a little. Yet neither France nor Germany has enjoyed thirty years of peace at any time within recent history. Neither country has been free from warlike operations on its own soil, while we have been entirely spared this form of devastation.

We have lost far more wealth from politics than

from wars, and it is because America gives little thought to either that the 117,000,000 Americans are in material comforts the most fortunate people in the world.

We are now threatened with another exposition of the political money folly in the Socialist surtax proposal, which, should it be put into effect, would once again upset all our calculations, but which, apart from financial inconvenience, would produce nothing.

The Socialists, by the way, will have to find a new name for their confiscatory proposals, since Mr. Churchill has stolen their word for his Super Tax complications.

The surtax is a side issue, and in that way does not differ from most political questions to-day. Political discussion has degenerated in recent times from doctrine to detail.

Some years ago I employed an American sales expert to manage the " subscription " travellers of one of my trade papers, " The Cabinet Maker." The method of this Yankee was ingenious. My travellers were gravely instructed in the trick of developing a discussion with a prospective customer as to whether he would prefer to have " The Cabinet Maker " from a local bookseller, or direct by post from the publisher. Elaborate arguments were developed, setting out the relative merits of the two systems of delivery. The other alternative —that the prospective customer should not buy " The Cabinet Maker " at all—was so skilfully ignored and evaded as to pass from the mind of the victim of the stratagem. For a time this finesse succeeded.

So it is with the Socialist surtax. Somebody suggests that it should apply to incomes of £500 and over. The debate becomes fast and furious on all the details. Why £500? Why a surtax? Why not increase the income-tax? Why not do it this way or that way? Nobody ever bothers even to think of the purpose or principles of taxation, the need for taxes, the use to which they are put, the good or the harm which they can do.

This is, of course, usual in politics. We fail, either through lack of ability or because we are too lazy to get a bird's-eye view of the problem with which we tinker so disastrously. One day we apply ourselves to railways, and put them in a position to ruin the mines. A few weeks or months later, when the miners complain, we forget the railways and talk about subsidies. We pass on, in our careless, irresponsible manner, to saddle ourselves with burdens on behalf of sugar beet, blind to the fact that we are already the largest consumers of sugar in the world. Having killed the sugar trade, we shall talk about the folly of capitalism or the madness of the other party.

Let any fool to-day propound a new way of undermining the prosperity of the nation and immediately each of the three political parties will hold a conference to expound their own pet scheme, not for getting rid of the fool but for giving effect to the folly.

It is just the same with the surtax. The Labour party makes a proposal on the assumption—which is allowed to go almost unchallenged—that more money must be found. We thus find ourselves plunged without more ado into the details of the taxes. No political party seems strong enough to say that no more money is wanted, that the way to success, national and individual, is to raise less money by taxation. And so, as alternative to surtax, the Liberals offer us death duties, and the Tories propose tariffs.

The surtax can be regarded from at least five different standpoints : (1) That of the taxpayer; (2) that of the dole receiver or tax beneficiary; (3) that of the Treasury; (4) that of industry; (5) that of the nation as a whole.

At present, however, the money fallacy dominates this country. It is not realised that if, by means of surtax, we levelled the incomes of all down to £500; if, when that were done, we all continued to do the same work as now; and if we gave all the surplus to the poor, we should not have gained an extra house or a single extra penny bun as the result of that operation. More houses and more buns are wanted, not more money.

By way of illustrating my contention, suppose that we take £1 from " A," the wealthy person, and give it to " B," the poor man. If, in consequence, " A " gives up cigars and " B " buys a pair of boots, the world may be a little better in that the health of both will be improved, that of " A " by the lack of cigars, that of " B " by the acquisition of boots. The wealth of the community as a whole remains unaffected. Four distinct things have been done :

    1. A man without boots has been satisfied if an extra pair of boots has been made.

    2. The bootmakers have received more wages.

    3. A cigar maker has gone out of work.

    4. If the man " B " is capable of making something with the proceeds of which he might have bought the boots and has failed to make that thing because of the above operation, then definite harm has been done.

However the problem is considered, the best that can be said is that in the most favourable circumstances wealth may be better distributed. It can never be claimed that any additional wealth is made by this sort of operation, and it is gravely to be feared that the total wealth is thereby reduced. Far too many people believe that money is omnipotent, that nothing can be done without it. It will place one man in a better position than another, and the moving of money may alter the relative positions of men, but money of itself will not add one iota to the real wealth of the nation.

In so far as the surtax will discourage or curtail saving it will quite definitely defeat its one object of relieving poverty. Examination of the figures of our staple industries shows that, for every worker employed, £1,000 worth of capital, machinery and equipment is required. The proportion is rather higher on the railways, but it may be taken as roughly true that every wage-earner requires £1,000 in bricks, mortar, machinery and tools to make his work effective. Every £1,000, therefore, taken off our savings as a nation adds one man or woman to the roll of the unemployed.

However much it may go against the grain, in our modern way of thinking, to leave the millionaire with his millions, we should not overlook the fact that the millionaire can do nothing with his money, directly or indirectly, but invest it in some sort of machinery which has to be worked by somebody. The cutting down of wealth by taxation, therefore, cuts off our supply of the capital upon which our industries and our wage-earners depend for their very existence.

Belonging, as I do, to the Gladstone school of finance, I believe that all our present poverty is directly due to taxation. To emphasise this point it is worth while to indulge in a fantastic exaggeration. Exaggeration sometimes helps in the search after truth. If it could be assumed that in November, 1918, when we signed a military armistice, we had also signed an economic armistice, that from that day to this we had had a ten-year holiday from Parliaments and bureaucrats, and that in consequence no money had been collected in taxes, then to-day there would be £10,000,000,000 in the pockets of private individuals ready for investment in industry, and to provide employment for ten million more workers at the rate of £1,000 per worker. In these impossible circumstances we should have arrived at the position when labour could secure any price it cared to demand, and when capital could be had for 1 per cent. per annum.

The surtax will not stop luxury-spending, but increase it. Excessive luxury, which so properly offends all right-thinking people, is due to the ease of profiteering in a restricted market brought about by the lack of capital which, in its turn, is caused by excessive taxation. My case is, therefore, against taxation rather than against any particular tax or surtax.

Contemplate the taxes we have got already! See what we have done in the last fifteen years in this way, and it must at once be obvious that our troubles arise not from the absence of a surtax, but from the presence of a super-tax and all the other official extortions.

In 1913 the taxpayer with an income of £100 a year paid about £6 in taxation; in 1923 he had to pay £15. In 1913 the taxpayer with £1,000 a year contributed £80 to the Exchequer; in 1923 £160. The levy on an income of £2,000 a year was £95 in 1913, against £331 ten years later; while in the same period the tax upon £20,000 a year has risen from £1,591 to £8,321. These figures apply if we reckon direct taxation only. The taxation per head of the population—and it is all too little appreciated that taxation is paid by the whole population in the price of commodities and not by the wealthy man who writes the cheque—was oppressive enough in 1913-14 at £4 6s. 5d. per head, but in 1926-7 at £18 12s. 6d. per head it is the root cause of our worst industrial ills.

I observed earlier that the surtax could be discussed from five different points of view, the first-mentioned being that of the taxpayer, and it would be useful if all parties would agree that he has no standing on personal grounds. Taxation is a question of the well-being of the entire nation, and the personal well-being of some particular class of individuals is quite beside the mark. It would clear the air considerably if we could all agree to give up the " What's mine's my own " line of thought.

Years ago John Morley wrote to Joseph Chamberlain : " No right is worth a straw apart from the good that it brings, and claims to right must depend not upon nature, but upon the good that the said rights are calculated to bring to the greatest number." If we argue—as, of course, I do—in favour of private property, we must do so because we believe private property to be in the public interest. It is the only basis upon which such property can be justified in this stage of the world's history. From the taxpayer's point of view, indeed, the surtax might bring, like so many economic ills, its own cure. Its sponsors have not considered the tremendous political consequences if everybody with £500 a year were subjected to the inquisitorial methods now reserved for the privileged 80,000 or 90,000 super-tax payers. The super-tax payer does not count as a political force, but two or three million £500-a-year people would have to be reckoned with.

Similarly, and secondly, the dole-receiver or the tax beneficiary is out of court. It is essential that we should not allow ourselves to impoverish the nation by thinking only of the individual position

of somebody who happens to want something.
There has been far too much "citizenship by
proxy." We have developed to extremes the art
of paying somebody else to spend the other man's
money. As to the dole-receiver's point of view,
there is another consideration which should not be
overlooked. We have among us to-day 1,000,000
people who have mastered the art of qualifying for
one or other of the several forms of benefit offered
by the State. Another million are waiting for new
benefits. We shall quickly reach a stage when the
chief occupation of the nation is filling up forms, on
the one hand in connection with the payment of
taxes, and, on the other, associated with the receipt
of relief.

Thirdly, the Treasury. I have no means of
knowing the official view, but there can be no question that the sensible Treasury view of this matter
must be for some simplification rather than for any
further complication of the taxing machine. A third
tax added to income-tax and super-tax means much
more expense in collection, and also means, of
course, much more evasion.

I have yet to find even the Socialist who will argue
that the surtax is designed to help industry. Industry wants capital, and a surtax will not assist it in
that way.

Thus we come down to the last point of view,
from which this taxation problem should be argued
—the point of view of the nation as a whole. It is
the last and the only relevant consideration. I do
not think that there would be much doubt on the

general question of taxation, or about any suggestion for increasing the national charge, if we could get our people to study, not so much where the money comes from, as where it goes.

We have agreed long enough ago that taxes should be placed upon the shoulders of those best able to bear them. We have committed ourselves irrevocably to the theory that the higher the income the higher the tax, and we have developed a position in which 43,000,000 people delude themselves into thinking that public expenditure is borne by the two millions who nominally pay the taxes.

If, however, we look at the matter the other way round, and think about the channels into which the money disappears, we get on to a more democratic basis, for while there may be differences of opinion as to who pays taxes, nobody will dispute that every pennyworth of public expenditure is undertaken with a view to the interests of the whole. Thus each of us as citizens, in theory at least, receives his proper share of the benefit from money spent from the public purse.

Now the public purse takes in and pays out, nationally and locally, no less a sum than £3 per week per family. I wish it were possible for every elector to get this vital point firmly fixed in his mind, disregarding altogether where the money comes from. No doubt can be entertained that £3 is spent every week in the name of, and on behalf of, every family in the land. If this question could be put squarely to every working-man elector: "Are you getting £3 value every week from all these Acts of Parliament, all these public authorities, and all these political blessings that are so freely showered upon you?" the answer would assuredly be emphatic, definite, and fatal to any proposals for further taxation. It is too much to hope that the modern working man will develop any considerable indignation at the robbing of the rich, so long as he is left with the impression that he himself derives some benefit from the process. But when at last he understands, as £3 a week would make him understand, that the benefits are not only vastly overestimated, but that, after all, he himself may be the victim of the robbery, another point of view will prevail.

CHAPTER VIII

THE BLESSING OF COMPETITION

WHAT is work? Why do we do it? Do we work because we like it or because we have to? Are we working for ourselves or for others? Is our real interest in our work or in the work of others who work for us? When the Government offers us a policy to promote employment, is it because we really want employment or because we want to qualify for a share in the product of the work of others?

We have as a people developed a political mind which is about as far removed as anything can be from what is practical and feasible in the everyday work of life. Thus, when a workman has a wife and five children, we argue about the cost of living. We never mention his work; we never ask if it is good work. We are not interested to know whether it could be better done or what is the opinion of the consumer for whom it is done. We do not even consider whether the work is worth doing at all. We merely repeat the cost-of-living figure, and think of the five children. We as a people approach the industrial problem in the attitude of mind which would be appropriate to a Board of Guardians, but which is simply destructive when applied to the problem of industry as a whole.

It would seem to be necessary to retrace our steps and to get back to the study of simple economics. I have already stated the old-fashioned object, as defined by Adam Smith, of " providing a plentiful subsistence for the people," and we must think not first of what the people want, but first of what there is for them to have. Secondly, how that which exists can be increased, and, thirdly, and only thirdly and lastly, of how this subsistence, plentiful or scarce as the case may be, can be made to satisfy the people's wants. To think in any other order must lead to disaster, and we are certainly thinking in the wrong order to-day. Our habit is, first to want something and then proceed to denounce, if not indeed to fight, the first convenient person or institution for failing to supply that want, without bothering to inquire whether the said person or institution has any sort of responsibility for the want or the absence of the means of supplying it, or any sort of power to solve the problem.

A perfect illustration of the political method, an illustration that is perhaps the more perfect because the politicians are not directly concerned, is to be found in the recent history of rubber and cotton. The rubber people, each of them presumably having a wife and five children, find that the price of rubber is inconveniently low to satisfy what they regard as their proper requirements. They therefore contrive, with the assistance of the Government in the Straits Settlements and our own Colonial Office, a scheme for the limitation of the output of rubber. This scheme works so satisfactorily as to cause the price of rubber in America to be doubled. The Americans, each of them having a wife and five children and thinking only of the cost of living, determine that something must be done to defeat the price of rubber and proceed to limit the output of cotton, in order to make its price proportionate to the rubber price.

This scheme, if successful, will reduce the amount of cotton available for the rest of us. That plan in its turn incommodes the cotton manufacturers of Lancashire, who, in the same way infected with the political mind, are each thinking of the cost of living and the wives and children. And so Mr. J. Maynard Keynes, the latest of the prophets of the new gospel of organisation, goes to Lancashire and devises a scheme for the limitation of the output of manufactured cotton. If this plan were to succeed, the rest of us would have to make one shirt do the work of two. Mr. Keynes, or one of his school, will then proceed to organise a scheme for the limitation of the output of laundry-work, which in its turn will involve the closing of some of the soap factories. So we shall have an ever-increasing number of organisations with ever-more complicated rules and regulations. We shall acquire more and more skill in the art of negativism and have an ever-diminishing quantity of things to eat and wear and use.

The rubber folly is mercifully coming to an end, and it is much to be hoped that its lesson will be widely and seriously studied. A few years of the Collectivist folly in this field alone has not, it is true, ruined society, but it has robbed us of immense blessings that might by now have been ours. Future generations will have all their floors, if not their streets, covered with rubber, but only when competition once more gets going in this market. Mean-

while the English share of the rubber trade of the
world has been reduced from 75 per cent. to 50 per
cent., and a few people, conspirators against competition, have become wealthy, while every one of
the rest of us is definitely poorer.

Hence I argue that we must start again to think
of economics and trade and industry in simple, elementary and fundamental terms.   I maintain that
competition is a blessing and not a curse.

There is no subject upon which the politician
waxes more eloquent, or through which he appeals
more successfully to that sloppy sentimentalism
which bids fair to ruin us, than the subject of competition.   We are invited to believe that competition
is a cruel and a wicked thing, and when we reach
the political peroration and hear about '' every man
for himself and the Devil take the hindmost,'' our
enthusiasm reaches its height.   We applaud, vote
and create new committees, and feel that we are
really getting on with the new world.   Is this really
so?

If the eloquence that is applied to misrepresenting the character of competition were applied to the
corresponding and analagous force of gravity, I do
not doubt that the same ignorant enthusiasm could
in time be developed on behalf of an effort to abolish
that also.   The cruelty of the physical force of
gravity is far worse than the supposed cruelty
of the economic force of competition.   From the
cradle to the grave gravity threatens us with destruction.

Poets and writers could do far better with gravity

than they can do with competition. It is directly opposed to the whole of the inspiration of upward and onward thought. All the emotions surrounding the thought of " Excelsior " are damped down by this horrid thing which the physicists identify for our destruction, and which is known as gravity. This analogy may sound frivolous, but the most superficial examination will show that it is nothing of the kind. Competition does cause inconveniences, but so does gravity, and just as the physical world is held together by this force, which imposes odd inconveniences, so the economic world is absolutely dependent upon the force of competition.

The modern habit of objection to competition arises from the modern political folly of thinking of only one side of trade and industry. We insist upon concentrating the whole of our attention upon the maker of an article, and forget altogether the other person or persons whose need of the article is the only excuse for the making of it or for the existence of the maker. Without competition no market would ever have come into being, and if the attempt to eliminate competition succeeded every market would wither and disappear. We should thus drift into forgetting one need after another. We should live simpler and harder and shorter lives, and generation by generation we should retrace our steps to barbarism and to Eden, all the time steadily reducing our numbers until eventually we all disappeared.

We must organise, we must amalgamate, but on

no account, say the Collectivists, must we compete. This unreasoning passion for organisation has, within the last few years, shovelled money into the pockets of the company promoters, and turned the "bucket" shop into a gold mine. But apart from that little bit of wealth-making on behalf of bucket shop proprietors, this anti-competition notion is a devastating notion which robs humanity in the most disastrous way. We have succeeded in producing a state of affairs in which two men are able to occupy a position the work of which could very well be done by one.

If we consider all those absurd federations with which we are afflicted, we find employers, merchants and manufacturers engaged in similar iniquity, restricting and restraining, striving to get wealth out of scarcity and plundering the rest of us after the fashion in which we have been dealt with in regard to rubber during the past few years. So firmly has this obsession got hold of the public mind that to-day, when we discover that it is possible to send messages by beam wireless, a commission is immediately set up to safeguard the cable companies from injury, and to see whether we may be permitted to enjoy the newly-found facilities of communication without damaging the interests of the old-fashioned cable. It would appear to be of much more importance, judging from these activities, that the cable companies should suffer no harm than that cheap means of communication should be made available to the public.

This nonsense about competition arises from the fact that we are thinking all the time of the producer and never of the consumer. The value of competition as a market maker is ignored; yet it is to competition that we owe every material amenity we possess. We have allowed public opinion on this question to become very seriously one-sided. In our endeavour to get rid of all that is meant by "wage slavery" we are forging chains of slavery for ourselves as consumers. But we are all of us much more directly interested in the economic position as consumers than as producers.

We have got away from that Victorian basis when we were producing wealth at a rate not only unprecedented in history but, having regard to the limited facilities at our disposal, altogether extraordinary.

We are faced with two alternatives. Either we must stand in the market place to be hired as producers, or stand in the queue to be rationed as consumers. By our preference in the past for the market-place we have produced an ever-increasing quantity of wealth for the benefit of the community as a whole. We have yet to be sure that the system under which we stand in the queue to be rationed will produce anything wherewith to support us. The tendency is for less and less to be produced.

That leads me further back still to another old Victorian thought, a thought which was never questioned fifty years ago, but is very seriously questioned to-day. "The buyer settles the price, an

article is worth what it will fetch, no more, no less."
That seems to me to be a truth which wants
preaching day and night, in season and out of
season, a truth from which we are in vain trying to
escape.

I am perfectly well aware that a superficial view
may not reveal this truth. When I, as a publisher,
for instance, produce a novel and put 7s. 6d. on the
cover, it looks as if I were fixing the price of the
novel at 7s. 6d. In one way I am doing so. But if
anyone thinks that is the whole truth he should visit
my warehouse and store-rooms and see the tons of
7s. 6d. novels for which no buyer will offer any
price. That is the melancholy fate of many novels
published to-day.

If we accept the theory that the buyer rules the
price, we will see that it explodes the ideas underlying most arrangements of the trade unions and of
federations and combines of all kinds. It throws a
vivid light on that modern abuse—the costing system. Karl Marx said that the price of a commodity
is equal to the cost plus the profit. He was, of
course, profoundly wrong—yet we have in this
country alone thousands of worthy people, who
would put their hands on their hearts and swear they
would never have anything to do with Socialism and
Communism, actually accepting the false definition
of Karl Marx.

One result of the present situation is the frightful
abuse of the science of cost accountancy. There
never was so bad a case of a blessing turned into
evil. Cost accountancy properly used—used as a

means of discovering economy—is a great blessing. Cost accountancy as commonly used to-day, to try in accordance with the Marxian formula to justify prices that no market will pay, is an abuse and a scandal. We used to talk of a willing buyer and a willing seller. A business transaction used to be tested by the simple formula : " Was it associated with a willing buyer and a willing seller? " We have long since passed the time when there was a willing buyer, and we have nearly obliterated the willing seller.

The philologists will have presently to note a very significant change that has crept over the meaning of the word "authority." This may be due to the copious use of the word in the 2,500 Acts of Parliament which have endeavoured to regulate and to curtail industrial matters in the first quarter alone of the twentieth century. Every other clause in these precious documents sets out how some " authority " shall " do " something. It may be an Imperial Minister, or it may be a minor local authority, but it is always an " authority."

Our every action has to be framed to ideas laid down by something which is called the " authority." It is really humorous to consider how the clerks in a parish council office, busy entering the wrong numbers in bad writing on some official form, are spoken of with awe and respect as " authorities." The practical builder, who spends his life acquiring a knowledge of the intricacies and technicalities of his trade, is, when mentioned by the rest of us, described in terms which imply a certain amount of derogation and contempt as a " trader," or, worse still, as a " private trader," or perhaps a " profiteer." But the second cousin of the Mayor, who, having failed to get into any useful or productive employment, is jobbed into a clerkship in the office of the borough surveyor, is dignified with the title of " the authority." If this same clerk, with his forms and licences, honours a building job with his presence, having travelled there in a municipal motor-car, the builder and the architect and the practical workers have to stand aside, almost remove their hats, and adopt an attitude of subservience to " the authority."

This illustration could be multiplied a thousand-fold. The relative positions of the householder who pays for the telephone and the young lady in the exchange on the permanent staff of the telephone " authority," will not bear a moment's serious economic consideration. When competition is eliminated real service disappears.

We must begin again to understand that authority is always a negative thing. It can say " don't," but it can never say " do." It is, for instance, possible for the police constable to make quite sure that Charlie Chaplin does not make a film, but it is not possible for a constable or even a sergeant to make sure that he does. Imperial Parliament can suppress a trade and, as in the case of the drug traffic, it is sometimes advisable to do so. But Imperial Parliament cannot, in any conceivable circumstances, create or promote trade as a whole. There

is not and never can be the slightest exception to
this rule.

It is, of course, perfectly true that by prohibiting
the import of bananas, Parliament can make it com-
mercially possible to grow bananas in greenhouses
in Birmingham, and the one or two people who
would be so employed may, in the narrowness of
their vision, form the impression that Parliament has
created a trade for them; but they forget that the
Government of Jamaica is likely to retaliate by prohibiting the import of the articles which previously
paid for the bananas. They also forget that whether
or not this happens, a banana does not take Acts of
Parliament into consideration in deciding where it
can grow, and that in limiting its choice of a nursery
in this way, its quantity and its productivity are
limited. The supply is diminished, its price en-
hanced, and the banana trade as a whole, considered
as a service to the people of the world as a whole, is
crippled, and the subsistence of the people as a
whole to that extent reduced.

But authority in these days extends very much
further down than Parliaments. We have myriads
of authorities, all suppressing competition and indi-
viduality, from the Prime Minister to the secretary
of the smallest trade union branch, every one of
them, in so far as they exercise their authority in the
realm of production, working to restrain output, restrict exchange, limit supply, and reduce the quantity of goods or services at the disposal of the rest of
us. The irony of the situation lies in the fact that
these restraints are generally imposed with the

ostensible object of removing poverty. They always, however, create more poverty than they cure, and the combined effect of all of them is to so reduce our capacity for wealth production as to accelerate the impoverishment of all.

CHAPTER IX

THE REAL CAUSE OF UNEMPLOYMENT

UNEMPLOYMENT has taken the place in politics left vacant by the disappearance of the Irish problem, and unless we acquire a better understanding of the matter than is evident at the moment, it may like the Irish question remain an ever growing trouble for generations to come.

There is no greater scourge associated with modern civilisation than the curse of unemployment. It is a terrible thing for the individual affected by it and a disgraceful thing from the point of view of society. I can conceive of no horror to equal that of the capable hard-working man unable, owing to circumstances over which he has no control, to find employment. But we can agree about that without agreeing as to causes and cures. We are far too prone to hold up both hands in support of any scheme proposed by any politician if only the proposal is labelled "unemployment." In point of fact we have created a great deal of unemployment by the measures that we have taken nominally to cure the evil, and so long as we go along on present political lines the chances are that we shall have more and more, instead of less and less, unemployment. Since the war, alone, three governments, Coalition, Labour and Conservative has exhausted the possibilities of State action with the direct result that year by year the amount of employment available for our people has steadily diminished.

Unemployment is an unnatural state of affairs which arises from an unnatural way of looking at things. In theory there can never be unemployment. So long as there is a want in the world there is work to be done, and as there will always be wants there will, therefore, always be work. But we have created an unnatural position by concentrating all our thoughts on the work instead of on the wants. We seem to think that there is some virtue in the work as work and give little or no thought to the wants which are, of course, the only conceivable excuse for the work at all. We have, in fact, got the picture upside down. We are looking through the wrong end of the telescope, and as long as we continue to do that the trouble will get worse and worse, and all hope of improvement will disappear.

If a wide view is taken, the problem of work and employment, looked at as a whole, is really very simple. Most big problems are simple; it is in the details that the difficulties arise. The whole world to-day may be said to be suffering from a surplus of labour and a shortage of wealth. There is a great deal of labour that is not utilised, and there is too little wealth to satisfy the legitimate desires of humanity. A surplus of labour and a shortage of wealth sums up, therefore, the whole situation.

In these circumstances the whole world—for the trouble is by no means confined to this country or this Empire—seems to be engaged in doing the wrong things. So thoroughly has the Socialist germ permeated society as a whole that all Governments, all authorities, all (or almost all) unions, associations and other Collectivist bodies, are busy all the time inventing new restraints, new restrictions, new prohibitions, limiting, if indeed they do not prevent, the making and the distribution of wealth. We ourselves pass two Acts of Parliament a week; every Government in the world follows our example; every trade union is day by day making new rules; every trade association devising new schemes, all of them arranging that something shall *not* be done. The whole world, being, as I think, quite mad in these matters, seems to be engaged in a determined effort to limit production. Everybody is seeking to make wealth out of scarcity.

If it were possible for these ideas to be discarded to-morrow, and for the whole world to agree that prosperity can only be secured out of production, a very short time, certainly not more than six months, would be required to reverse the economic position everywhere and to produce a state of affairs in which there would be a shortage of labour and a surplus of wealth. Then, as I have already shown in the chapter on money, labour could secure almost any price it cared to ask, and the return on capital would be reduced to a mere fraction of the present rate of interest. But the unemployment problem cannot, unfortunately, be tackled in that broad and general way; we can only strive to put public opinion right, and public opinion will in time put the problem right. To-day, however, we have to do something, or, maybe, have to undo something, in order to relieve the smaller and immediate troubles which we find on our own doorstep.

There is another big general consideration which must be noted in passing. Unemployment is a very valuable political asset. I shudder to contemplate the plight of any one of our political parties if by some miracle we could wipe out unemployment from amongst us. Politicians, in my view, are between them mainly responsible for such unemployment as we have; but that does not prevent them from mounting their respective platforms and blaming the unfortunate business man, the Capitalist system, or anybody or anything but the real culprits and the real causes. The politicians, therefore, will always make the most of unemployment; that is in the nature of things. There is to-day a most sinister attempt on the part of seekers after the sweets of office to develop an unemployment problem in America.

Many people are still under the impression that there are more than a million persons who in former, normal, ordinary times were properly employed, but who now, owing to the war, to the state of the world, to the breakdown of Capitalism, or to other causes glibly explained by the politicians, cannot find work.

This impression is wholly false, although it is sedulously promoted by the politicians. The word "unemployment" no longer means "absence of work." It would more correctly be defined as "qualification for benefit." The million people about whom the politicians talk are not for the most part people who have lost work which existed before, but are merely people who have fitted themselves into the political arrangements which we have thought well to make in the name of unemployment.

If the State devises benefits and offers them to its citizens it cannot complain if its citizens proceed to put themselves into a position to claim the benefits.

So much for general considerations. Now for detail. There is a garage at a well-known seaside resort which in the summer employs fifty men. A holiday-making public pays those fifty men for six or seven months of the year on a generous scale, which is justified, or tolerated, on the theory that a whole year's living has to be picked up in a short holiday season. Prior to the introduction of un-employment insurance these men either lived upon the earnings of six or seven months' work or else found, for five or six months, casual engineering work to keep them going. The habit of the garage ever since it was established has been to cut its staff down to ten or fifteen men during the winter season.

When I last visited that garage, just after Christmas, thirty-five members of its staff were drawing the dole. This may be good; it may well be argued that a beneficent State has made arrangements which have removed a social injustice, but that is something very different from what is understood by ordinary people when the word "unemployment" is used. There is here no breakdown of Capitalism, no abnormal circumstance, no bad trade, nothing, in fact, which has not always happened before.

When the million unemployed are analysed in this way it will be found that there is in point of fact as much employment to-day as ever there was, and in my view there would be much more employment still, but for the meddling and the muddling of the politicians. The remedy for unemployment is not to devise new sorts of relief, but to study the causes and remove them.

There are, of course, a million people drawing unemployment benefit, but to arrive at a true comparison of the position to-day and the normal position it is impossible to accept the million figure. Many adjustments must be made in studying this supposed million. To begin with, a very large deduction must be made on account of the women. It is not only a question of the few odd thousand women who are drawing unemployment money. We must also reckon the millions of women who were pushed into industry during the war, who formed no part of the industrial army in the normal times before the war and who are now occupying places which were previously held by men. Then we must deduct from the million all the juveniles who in normal times were left, and as I think rightly left, to the care of their families, but who are now taught to look to the beneficent State almost from the moment that they leave school.

Thirdly, from the million must be subtracted all the seasonal and occasional workers, like the garage hands to whom I have referred. These people are an army in themselves. The worst class that I know so far as this problem is concerned is the sea-faring class. Periods of unemployment are part and parcel of the seaman's life, and, indeed, essential to it. A man puts to sea for a few weeks or a few months in order to enjoy a period of leisure on shore, but now our seamen are discharged at the docks with a month or two's wages in their pockets, only to go straight to the Labour Exchange to register as unemployed, and to draw appropriate benefits until in the normal way they see fit to sign on to another ship.

Still larger corrections to the million figure are necessary on account of all those trades which have arranged their affairs so as to fit into the unemployment Acts. A flagrant illustration of this class of abuse is the cotton trade. Cotton has always had its periods of short time. The nature of the trade, depending upon a season's crop, has caused the cotton industry to be working sometimes at high pressure, sometimes at low pressure, and it is to be presumed that the economics of the cotton trade have been so arranged as to make the industry balance, having regard to these natural circumstances. The cotton trade, however, was not long in discovering that some slight rearrangement enabled its members to qualify for a Government subsidy in the form of unemployment pay, and where in normal times six weeks of short time would have been arranged, to-day masters and men conspire together to work three weeks of full time, thus qualifying for three weeks of dole.

These are only illustrations which could be multiplied almost indefinitely, but when the million is adjusted after taking all these matters into consideration, it is undoubtedly the fact that employment, whether it be good or whether it be bad, is to-day better than ever it was before.

If from the small residue of unemployment which is left when all these adjustments have been made we deduct the special case of coal, we begin to get the problem down to its proper proportions and to see that we ought to be talking about our prosperous condition and not about our impoverishment. Coal is a thing by itself, and the reader should never forget that when talking about coal he is referring to something which consists of 95 per cent. politics and 5 per cent. coal. For fifty years or more coal has been the favourite diversion of the politician. No industry has been subjected to more interferences, more regulation and more legislation. Millbank and Whitehall are full of coal departments. There are more bureaucrats in coal than there are in housing. I, therefore, do not hesitate to charge the politicians with the full responsibility for the plight of the coal industry.

Can anyone calculate how many unemployed and how much unemployment is due to trade union rules which force two men into one job? We all know how this stupidity arises. If the problem is taken in detail instead of as a whole, it even seems a sensible thing to do. One job offers, and must be done, and if two men can screw wages out of it, why not? But such an argument overlooks the fact that a dozen other jobs of the same kind simply decline to come into the market so long as it is governed by such foolish rules and regulations.

Similarly, how much unemployment, I wonder, is caused by the folly of employers in adopting the policy of reducing wages, inculcating into the minds of workers the notion that the less they do the better off they will be? Or again, can anyone say how much work is killed at the source by the two Acts of Parliament a week which it has been our habit to pass all through my lifetime.

A great deal of unemployment arises from the stupid, common talk about good trade and bad trade. Politicians in particular are very fond of talking in this way. The notion seems to be that trade is like manna which drops from heaven. The sooner we get rid of that idea the better. Trade is what we make it. Trade goes to the efficient. Trade will be good if only we are determined to get on with the job.

No discussion of unemployment would be complete without reference to another very serious side of the question. I refer to the huge vested interest of the bureaucracy. Herbert Spencer told us all about it in " The Coming Slavery," and every word he wrote in that pamphlet has proved true. We established, as I think very foolishly and very unwisely, a Ministry of Labour for the purpose of finding us work. That Ministry, from the moment of its birth to the present day, has failed in its purpose, a failure which does not surprise me seeing that the purpose is an unnatural one. The State cannot find us work; that is a job which we must do for ourselves.

But notice the rapidity with which we have discovered, in this case, that political action leads to the opposite effect to that desired. This great institution, with its enormous annual budget, founded to find us jobs, is now depending for its very existence on the absence of the jobs that it was established to find.

I have suggested that unemployment is due to an unnatural way of looking at things and I finish on that note.   When we consider how, in these modern days, we have ceased to take any account of the consumer; when we remember that all our talk is of work, employment, wages, hours, conditions, pensions, and anything but the object of the work itself, the product, or the consumer, the marvel is that any employment exists at all.   We depend, of course, all of us, upon the pleasure and satisfaction that we are able to give to others.   We work for no other reason than to supply the wants of others, and if we could get back to a full realisation of all that that means, and devote our minds to the endeavour to find new ways of serving others, then the problem would not be how to find employment, but how to find enough people to fill the employment that offered.

Unemployment, except in respect of a very small minority of unemployables, would disappear to-morrow if we could do two simple things.   First, dismiss the preposterous and degrading claim of the politicians to perform the impossible, and, second, secure a general acceptance of the old truth, now almost forgotten, that we live by rendering service to others, and that civilisation can be maintained in no other way.   That is the gospel of Individualism. It forces on to each of us a full sense of our personal responsibility.   It develops in the breast of each of

us that spirit of endeavour and independence which
makes for progress, and it is the exact opposite of
the Socialistic notion that we have a lot of rights
which the State must deliver, a notion which is
simply breeding a dependent race, undermining the
strength of the nation, and must continually reduce
us to lower and lower levels. We are still progress-
ing because there is still more Individualism than
Socialism, but progress which is slower than it
should be is really not progress at all.

CHAPTER X

THE BURDEN OF BUREAUCRATS

WE are all democrats but we know little enough about democracy and from appearances we seem to care even less.

When a body of people, a society, a town, or a nation decide to take some action collectively they do not themselves take that action, but always employ somebody else to undertake it for them. A town appoints a town clerk, an association appoints a secretary, a nation appoints officials in the various departments of Government. These people are in every case the servants of those who appoint them; that, at least, is the theory of the matter. We always speak of public *servants* and of the public *service*. But things do not work out that way in practice. Theory and practice have a nasty habit of differing, and public servants all too often become, in fact, public masters.

Perhaps the biggest political problem of the age, which, like all really big problems, is not much discussed, is the slow, sure, steady, silent transference of power into the hands of our new masters—the bureaucracy. Self-government is a very difficult thing to get and a still more difficult thing to work. The democratic principle is the basis of our liberties, and, as I have said before, the democratic principle is in danger. It will be a sad conclusion to the glorious history of the British Constitution if, having through the centuries wrested power from one privileged class after another until all power is quite definitely placed in the hands of the people, the people should now proceed to relinquish that power into the hands of the new privileged class, worse in every way than any of those that have gone before—the bureaucratic class.

We must, of course, have a certain amount of Government. The most bigoted Individualist recognises the need for Justice, Defence and Education, as well as for roads and drains and a few other things which, at whatever cost, can only be secured through collective action. But to argue, as the Socialists do, that because the roads are publicly owned, therefore everything else should belong to the public, is at best a failure to appreciate the difference between necessity and convenience.

There are two ways of looking at Government. Some people seem to regard it as a blessing which must be encouraged and developed and increased in every possible way. Others, and this is surely the more sensible view, look upon Government as an expensive and necessary evil, of which a free and enlightened people should have as little as possible.

It is easy to show that those things which are done by public authority, even when they are well done, are the subject, and must always be the subject, of gross extravagance, waste and delay. That is not because Civil Servants are incompetent, but because things which are done in the name of the public must be done with meticulous regard to order and procedure. Public action offers more opportunities for abuse than private action, but it would be wrong in this country, though not in others like America, to attack public action on the grounds of abuse.

I came across a particularly flagrant case quite recently, but I do not pretend that it is typical. Public parks must, of course, be owned and maintained by public authority, and I was walking through one of the London parks only a day or two ago. I stood and watched a uniformed gardener, beautifully clothed, reminding one of the dustman in William Morris's "News from Nowhere." His boots and gaiters were polished and nowhere about him was a sign of business contact with Mother Earth. He wore gloves, and in his right hand was a small pair of sécateurs. He was standing beside an old laurel bush, taking in his left hand one leaf at a time and snipping it off with the implement in his right hand. By the side of him there stood yet another public official, also a gardener and also arrayed in all the beauties of the London County Council uniform. This fellow was holding a sack, into which his companion leisurely deposited one at a time the old laurel leaves as he cut them from the bush. Three or four yards away on the path was a third official, obviously of a lower grade, because he wore no uniform, sitting on an empty barrow, waiting for the sack when it might, in due time, have received its quota of old laurel leaves.

I do not put this forward as an example of what happens in most of our public work, but it may fairly be said that this sort of abuse is only possible when collective action is taken on such a scale as to wipe out all trace of individual responsibility.

I understand that the windows of Windsor Castle are cleaned on the inside by the Office of Works and on the outside by the Department of Woods and Forests. This may be inevitable if these things are to be done at all with public money, for public money must be spent in accordance with well-defined public principles.

We have allowed the business of Government to grow to enormously swollen proportions, until to-day we are putting into the hands of the bureaucrats, national and local, no less a sum than a £1,000,000,000 a year. Nobody will, therefore, question the wisdom at this stage of a pause for consideration, nor will anyone think it unwise if we now ask ourselves how far all this expenditure is really worth while, and whether the tendency of the future should be to increase or to diminish it.

There are four kinds of bureaucrat, or quasi-bureaucrat; four distinct classes that have grown out of our enthusiasm for political or Collectivist action. First we have the bureaucrats proper, national and local, hundreds of thousands of them taking their salaries direct from the public purse. Secondly, there is an enormous bureaucracy which has fastened itself on to the trade union movement. The working-class contributions to trade union funds are very largely spent in the upkeep of an ever-growing class of officials, many of them having no other excuse for existence than the necessity for conferring with the public officials; and each class encourages the other to grow. Thirdly, the trade associations, which are the joint product of trade unionism and legislation, have provided themselves within quite recent times with a very big and rapidly growing bureaucracy of their own. Lastly, there are the lawyers and accountants who earn a living by explaining to the ordinary man all the sophisticated technicalities imposed upon him by the bureaucrats of all the other kinds.

Ever since the beginning of the century Parliament has passed two Acts of Parliament a week, 100 Acts a year, or nearly 3,000 Acts in all, each of them placing new restrictions on our liberty, and each of them calling for more bureaucrats to see that we behave in the manner required, and more lawyers to tell us how it is possible to act in the unnatural way which these legislative devices always prescribe. We must have in the neighbourhood of a million bureaucrats, a hundred thousand trade union officials, a hundred thousand association bureaucrats, and goodness knows how many lawyers and accountants, none of the whole of this huge army producing anything, and most of them making it more difficult for the rest of us to produce that which we must perforce share with them.

Between them they have created so unnatural a position that a large proportion of the brains which should be applied to the normal work of the world is diverted to the difficult task of complying with their requirements. The bureaucrat, very naturally, has a minor interest in the work over which he is set;

his chief interest is found in the technicalities of his own unnatural requirements. These people tend to get a completely false conception of their usefulness and their position. To them technical compliance with some clause of some Act of Parliament is much more important than, say, the building of a house. This interest in the machinery of bureaucracy leads naturally and easily to the development of bureaucratic abuse. Every reader will be able to supply illustrations from his own experience.

There was a time when one could be born with a single certificate, when an entry by the Registrar of Births and Deaths was sufficient compliance with the requirements of the bureaucrat to enable us to enter the world; but to-day we are not properly born until we are doubly registered, once for the benefit of the hoards of officials who keep the census and a second time for the information of the new legionaries of the Ministry of Health.

The interest of the official is in the sub-clauses of the Act of Parliament and in devising machinery which shall bring them out of their obscurity. His whole mind tends to become occupied with things that really do not matter.

I have upon occasion to write to the local authority of the district in which I live, and, being old and lazy, I find it difficult to pick out the many departments and the numerous officials and to decide exactly where the functions and prerogatives of each begin and end. My practice, therefore, is to write to the Clerk of the Council, just as in business one would write to the secretary of a company; but whereas in the latter case the secretary will pass the communication on to the appropriate department for immediate attention, in the former case a much more elaborate procedure has to be adopted.

In a somewhat lengthy experience I have never failed to get back from the Clerk of the Council a typewritten letter, duly copied and filed and posted under a three half-penny stamp, to inform me that he, the Clerk, has passed my letter over to the Surveyor, the Inspector, the Collector, the Regional Director, the Assessor, or whoever the other appropriate functionary may be. In this way this particular local authority is filling up building after building with more and more clerks as week by week Parliament provides it with more and more functions.

It should never be forgotten that from the nature of the case none of these people have, or can ever have, any interest in economy; they have nothing to gain and everything to lose from any such idea. When I was an amateur bureaucrat at the Ministry of Munitions, my little department did its very best to increase its personnel. Seventy-five persons gave me the right, as head of the department, to a carpet and an armchair, while my secretary could then claim a desk with drawers down the sides and in addition a mirror to hang on the wall. Economy must always be against the interests of the bureaucracy : two striking illustrations are on my desk as I write.

In the year 1919 I established *Ways and Means*,

a weekly review, and in that connection the Stationery Office sent me a daily list of official publications. In the same way I was put upon the list of the American Department of Labour in Washington, and the bureaucrats there were good enough to send to me from week to week a budget of official publications dealing with American industry. That was nearly ten years ago. *Ways and Means* died eight years ago, but that does not matter to the bureaucrats, either English or American, and I went on receiving the daily communication from the Stationery Office until I called their attention to the matter in the latter part of 1928, while the weekly budget from the Department of Labour at Washington still lumbers up my post box. In the same way our own Ministry of Labour goes merrily on to this day wasting its printed matter on the editor of the long-defunct *Ways and Means*.

It is very important that we should understand that a bureaucracy multiplies and increases in a way that is not given to institutions of any other kind.

I chanced upon a striking illustration of this some few days ago, when I found the father of three clever daughters boasting that each of them was making good progress in the study of medicine, and that all three were likely to become doctors. The father's pride seemed to me somewhat lacking in balance, as I have yet to learn that there is an unlimited market for feminine medical practitioners, and I put this point to him. His reply was definite, emphatic and confident. He did not for a moment imagine that these girls would earn a living in the medical market as doctors in search of a practice, "but," said he, "there will be more and more appointments for various sorts of inspectors." He was delightfully vague about it, but as he was in touch with the Ministry of Health he did not doubt that he could place all three. Here, surely, is a flagrant case where we are actually breeding bureaucrats.

It must not be supposed, as one would imagine from the study of the theory of democracy, that the people with one mind decide upon some urgent piece of work and then proceed to find some bureaucrat willing to undertake it. That is only the theory of the matter. In practice things happen exactly the other way round. These bureaucrats spend a large part of their time in drafting new sorts of legislation, which are pumped into Parliament through Ministers, passed without discussion and then forced upon the rest of us. Nobody can pretend that most of the financial and industrial legislation of the last decade or two has arisen from a conscious public demand. It has, of course, been invented and promoted by an interested bureaucracy. These people are our real rulers.

The lengths to which we have gone in this way can be seen by anyone who will take the trouble to read an ordinary daily newspaper. The summary of the news of the day as given in *The Daily Telegraph* of the day on which I am writing contains twenty items, which I was at some pains to analyse.

I found that three of these items were concerned
with the normal activities of ordinary, normal
people, acting on their own individual responsibility. The other seventeen items catalogued as
the day's activities were concerned entirely with the
antics of the various sorts of bureaucrats. There
were parliaments, councils, conferences, unions,
associations, commissions, inquiries, committees
and soviets of every sort, kind and description, one
of them suppressing the traffic in women and the
other sixteen suppressing almost every other kind
of trade and traffic ever thought of.

The public does not seem to recognise that these
bureaucratic arrangements are really designed to
hinder and not to help. Their authors would not,
perhaps, admit this, and Parliament seems to be
quite ignorant of this obvious characteristic. Take
a very simple illustration. The public will is that
a man who sells 15oz. and calls it a pound shall be
put in gaol as a thief, and the old-fashioned public
were content to rely upon the police force to catch
such a thief and to put him into gaol; but the bureaucrat has found a better method. He says that nobody may sell a pound until some bureaucrat has
been paid a salary to certify that it is not 15oz.
This arrangement provides a comfortable occupation for large numbers of inspectors, hinders not
only the thief who wishes to palm off 15oz. as a
pound, but everybody in the whole realm of business who under the bureaucratic blight is officially
branded as a thief until, by means of forms and

stamps and ceremonies, he has established his reputation for honesty.

No word of mine must be taken as implying any disrespect or lack of appreciation for officials as individuals. I number many of them among my personal acquaintance, and there is no more hard-working, conscientious, or well-meaning class amongst us. I take leave, however, to question whether the status and quality of the Civil Service will stand the strain of the recent introduction of hoards of the school board type. It must, or so it seems to me, be very distressing to professional Civil Servants to see their high calling degraded by the additions of legions of lower and middle-class people in the way that has happened in recent years.

My objection to the bureaucrat is of another kind. So long as he is concerned with those limited restraints which are a proper part of the business of government, he is in his proper place, doing his proper work and rendering a valuable service to society. But he must realise that his profession is to restrain, that he can do nothing else and that from the very nature of the thing he can be nothing but a nuisance and a hindrance when productive work is in question or normal human activity is desired.

The effect upon the standard of living of all of us of the inordinate growth of the bureaucracy and all the lesser bureaucracies is, of course, extremely serious. We are creating to-day an ever-growing number of non-producers, who have a claim to share the good things of life with an ever-diminishing number of the producers of those things. Individualism brings each of us into closer touch with production, while any other system tends to make more and more of us into parasites.

CHAPTER XI

EDUCATION AS A VITAL FORCE

WHEN discussion is concerned with industry or property like mines, or railways, or land, there is always plenty of material for the quarrel between Individualism and Socialism. In these cases there are conflicting personal interests, and champions will therefore always be found for different points of view. When, however, we come to subjects like education and health the case is different. These are helpless, abstract, intangible things which offer unlimited scope for the practice of Collectivist folly, almost entirely free from criticism or even examination. Education must always be recognised as a public service, and must therefore be nationalised or socialised. Private interests in education are now in the minority, and whatever one does with it no great questions, such as divide men into classes and parties, are likely to arise.

In education Collectivism has a real chance to show what it can do, because we have long ago accepted compulsory education, and everybody agrees that public authority in some form or another must undertake the administration of the educational machine. This being the accepted view, money has been showered into education in the most liberal and extravagant way. Every politician, at some time or another, pays lip service to the cause of economy, but few politicians of any party at any time dare to suggest that there should be any economising when the question is education.

Thus it comes about that while in 1914 our bill

for education was £19,169,647, we are to-day spending, nationally and locally and privately, in various forms of education, well over five times that sum. Collectivism never had such a chance as in this field. Nobody dares to breathe a word about saving money; there is not a suggestion anywhere of the use of private enterprise; there is no syllable of profit in the whole of the literature of education; it does not contain a vestige of Capitalism, and, of course, there is, in its administration, no trace of that modern horror which is labelled "competition." Education, therefore, is fair ground for testing and analysing Collectivist methods and ideas, studying their weaknesses and judging the results which accrue from them.

Whitaker's Almanack, the most congested and condensed work of reference we have, contains no fewer than forty-one pages of lists of educational authorities and institutions.

For fifty years public enthusiasm has been given whole-heartedly to the cause of education, and now we have 43,000,000 people upon whom the blessings of Socialism, as applied to education, have been freely bestowed. What are the results? What have we secured? How far have our aims and objects been attained? Are our people educated people? Can we notice qualities and characteristics in them which were lacking in their grandfathers who had no such education? These surely are not unfair questions to ask at this stage.

In my business capacity I receive from time to time applications for employment, and these applications set out as a rule a list of qualifications which will fit the applicant for the post applied for. It is very noticeable that if a man or woman has been fortunate enough to escape the public education machine he or she makes a great song about it when applying for a situation. Not only the universities and the great public schools, but all the minor private educational institutions are set out in large type with emphasis as evidence of the applicant's quality and abilities. But in thirty-five years as an employer I have never known a boy or girl claim employment on the grounds that they were educated by the London County Council, or the public authority of their locality, wherever it may be.

There are, of course, exceptions. I know of several secondary schools which have been able, in spite of the weight of officialdom under which they labour, to develop a certain amount of school *ésprit de corps*. This is, perhaps, more noticeable in the case of girls' than of boys' schools, probably because the teaching profession seems to be more attractive to the best type of woman than to the best type of man. But on the whole it must be confessed that public enthusiasm for spending money on education produces in the educated none of that sense of pride and possession which Socialists blather about, which we are assured would alter the whole spirit of the coal industry or any other trade to which it was applied. I feel that to many working-class families the seven years of compulsory education appear something like a period of conscription, if not a period of imprisonment, which has to be suffered and ended as soon as possible.

But what have we got in the way of education? And here I disclaim any desire to debate the vexed and difficult problem as to what is education. I am simply concerned to know how far this huge machine does produce the goods set out in the catalogue. We have drifted so far away from the old three R's that there are 40,000,000 of us who, taken as a whole, certainly cannot spell, whose caligraphy for the most part would pass no examination at all, and who find some mental compensation for arithmetical incompetence in a cynical boast that we have minds above such sordid detail. All that may or may not be good, but nobody can deny that if our £100,000,000 a year is spent in respect of reading, writing and arithmetic we are wasting most of our money. We can certainly dance, but not one in five hundred of us can speak the King's English.

As a publisher I may be prejudiced, but I always think I am entitled to complain that our educational expenditure has not produced a book-loving public. We are the worst-read nation in the civilised world. We produce and buy far fewer books per head than either America, France, or Germany and are even left beaten by Czechoslovakia.

It is, perhaps, hardly fair to go too low in the social scale in this business of testing the efficiency of our educational machine, but vast masses of us pass through that machine without receiving any benefit whatever. As president of the East End

Hostels Association it is my privilege to be in some sense responsible for a number of boys who lack a decent home, and when I talk to these boys I cannot escape a sense of astonishment that public money should have been squandered upon them for seven years or more without, so far as I can discover, in most cases a trace of effect. They are not bad boys; they possess all the characteristics and wonderful qualities which are to be found in almost every boy. We in our Association discover the raw material for all sorts of useful activities, and yet the socialised education machine has left them untouched.

Similar reflections must occur in the mind of anyone who is closely acquainted with the personnel of a large factory. Whatever our educational lavishness may do for the bright exception here and there, it seems to leave the mass with a more or less pleasant recollection of a wasted period of life and nothing else.

The educational institutions of this country are, as I have said, on a perfect Socialist model. We have small local bodies responsible to larger local bodies, who in their turn have to give account to one great central authority. There is the Socialist ideal of central finance and central control, a curse which, to the Individualist, is enough to murder any institution however heavenly its purpose.

This central control has been developed, as central control is always developed, through finance. We are at the moment in grave danger of an extension of this abuse from the proposal to relieve rates from the Exchequer, thus taking more large slices of responsibility out of the localities and opening wide the flood gates of extravagance and waste. Three-quarters of all the money for county education is supplied from taxes, and doled out through the Exchequer, while one-quarter only comes from local rates.

Thus we have achieved in education an almost complete absence of a sense of personal interest or local responsibility. It is pure folly that it should be so, because the localities pay the taxes just as much as the rates, but the effect of the central fund is to give to every locality the feeling that the money spent is not really a direct burden upon it.

We can be thankful that education, for its own sake, is so worth while that it will always attract wise and good men and women. Thousands of these wonderful people, merely for the joy they get out of the life of service in education, are prepared to face the ignominy and oblivion which are inseparable from a huge governmental socialised machine. There are no careers in education; Socialism has wiped all that out. There is still, of course, a headmastership of Eton, with a few dozen positions of similar importance and possessing similar attractions, but the headmaster of a secondary school has about the same social status and importance as that of the local police inspector.

This is not because the public like to look upon the headmaster in that sort of way, but because the educational Frankenstein so envelops him that he cannot be picked out and treated with the dignity and consideration that would be his in any more sensible educational arrangement. If in a general knowledge paper students were asked to name six great men in education to-day I doubt whether such a question would be answered by one per cent. of the examinees.

The word " education " really means, in modern language, " money for bureaucrats." If this may be thought to be an exaggeration, I refer the reader to the literature of education. Three-quarters of all the print and of all the speeches that are made in the name of education is concerned with the interests of teachers, their salaries, their status, their conditions of employment, their pensions, and so on. It is our old friend, the same trouble which we have noted in considering industrial problems, the public habit of getting the picture upside down. The teaching profession is brought down to the level of the bricklayer or the dock labourer. Most of our discussions are concerned with the interests of the producers, to the exclusion of the well-being of the consumers.

The cause of the teachers is a good cause. In many cases they are underpaid and cannot give us what we want in the conditions in which they have to work. But they are going the wrong way to achieve their ideals. They are acting just as the miners or the bricklayers or the railwaymen act, quite forgetting that the only excuse for their existence is the pupils whose interests they are there to serve. If they will concentrate their thoughts on him or her and, in the language of commerce, "produce the goods," they will be taking the quick road to the achievement of their own personal ends. It is all a misunderstanding of the doctrine of service, or the deep and inevitable workings of economic purpose. Collectivist power applied to education is dissolved in money, and that, of course, is what always happens to Collectivist power. We are standardising and stereotyping inefficiency and failing altogether in our pursuit of educational ideals.

What a different picture we get if we turn to America. It is not usual to look to America for light and leading in the matter of education. The Americans are not considered to be an educated people, but we find in America a determined enthusiasm for real education which is sadly lacking here. Perhaps it may be that the Americans are more conscious of their want of education, but no one can deny their unparalleled desire as a people to develop and improve themselves.

"The latest figures available," I quote from *Colombus Undergraduate*, "give the number of students enrolled in the universities, professional schools, and similar institutions as 726,000. More than 500,000 are members of the universities and colleges proper, of which there are 644 out of the 913 institutions that report to the U.S. Bureau of Education. On a geographical basis, 172 universities are situated in New England and the middle Atlantic States, while the southern States contain 139. Throughout the central and western States the universities number 333, of which 34 are distributed on the Pacific coast.   At least one, and on an average three, institutions in each State are under public control, and in 1926 more than $150,000,000 (£30,000,000) was provided out of the taxes towards their upkeep.   Private endowments are said to total about $550,000,000 (£110,000,000), Harvard University alone commanding about $70,000,000 (£14,000,000).   By way of comparison with England, it has been computed by one observer that the students in America number twenty times as many, among a population between twice and three times as great.   In Iowa alone there are as many university institutions as in England, though the population of this State is only 2,000,000: the largest of these has more students than either Oxford or Cambridge.''

The method of approaching the educational problem in America is, as might be expected, quite different from ours.   The U.S. Federal Government has nothing, or practically nothing, to do with education.   It runs a bureau, collects and distributes a few statistics, but leaves the main responsibility for the education of its people to the forty-eight States which constitute the great American confederation.   These forty-eight States enjoy educational autonomy; they all adopt the principle of compulsory education, but none of them depends on assistance or hindrance from central authority.   There is fierce competition amongst them for the honour of doing better than the rest in connection with education.   The result is that the country is swarming with universities, some of

them public but most of them private, all fighting
for the premier position, and education in that wonderful land enjoys the blessing which is denied to
us, the greatest of all human blessings, the blessing
of competition.

I wonder if it would be possible to shift the
Socialist and Individualist controversy over to education? Such a procedure might be for the good of
both Socialists and Individualists. We could get
a clearer issue in connection with education than we
can with coal mines. The argument would be free
of vested interest, and there would be no cause for
mistrust or misunderstanding. We could discuss
the relative merits of the two systems without heat
and with serious intellectual intent on both sides.

I should argue that the first step in the cure for
our educational shortcomings is to shut up Whitehall and to let the counties assume complete responsibility for the education of their own people. Let
the spirit of competition enter into this great cause.
If the counties were conscious of their personal
responsibility and understood what they don't
understand to-day, that in any case they are spending their own money, the result would be not
a set back—that would never happen—but an out-
pouring of wealth and enthusiasm which has never
yet occurred in this country.

Let us give to the local lights of places like
Dorset and Essex a chance to shine without the
shadow of the great panjandrum from Whitehall to
dim them. We have an enormous asset, a vitally
powerful force of which we make little or no use,

in local patriotism. The pride of citizenship, which is the most precious thing to be found in most of our small cities, gets little chance to apply itself to education. It does wonders with hospitals, and would do greater wonders with education. It cannot be denied that every county is interested in the quality of its boys and its girls, and yet that interest has to-day no encouragement and no opportunity to find a practical outlet.

The life of a teacher would be a very different thing if the county enthusiasm were behind his work. Would it not, for instance, be possible to link up county education with county sport? The divorce of sport from public education, a divorce which is inevitable in any national scheme, is one of the greatest of the tragedies in our great educational blunder.

The subject is a big one and I can do no more than touch upon it in a single chapter. It is, strange to say, a new subject, because we have allowed the education monster to develop almost without discussion. But it is a useful subject to help us with this bigger problem of Individualism versus Socialism. If it is even suspected, and I think it is proved, that educational endeavours are failing in their purpose because of the lack of the vital force of competition, then we shall indeed have moved a long way forward towards a better understanding of most of our economic difficulties

CHAPTER XII

HOUSING

THE building trade and housing market furnish perhaps the best field in which to study the evils of Collectivism. Ever since Mr. Lloyd George introduced his People's Budget and the famous Form IV. there has been no room for a vestige of Individualism, and the speculative builder and the small house-owner, who between them provided most of the houses we have, are practically things of the past.

The housing question is a vast medley of false facts, muddled thinking and political chicanery.

In discussing the housing problem, therefore, it is desirable first of all to deal with some wholly false notions which seem to have fastened themselves upon the public mind. The first of these is that which deals with the first appearance of a slum. It is all too commonly supposed that in the days when the factories were appearing in the towns a class of person, not at all clearly defined, set out of evil purpose to build houses of inferior materials and unhealthy design, and that the workers, in some way which is never explained, were forced into these hovels by the same evil persons.

Surely nothing could be farther from the truth. The houses which we of the twentieth century, with our greater knowledge, now regard as inadequate and call slums were, at the moment of their building, literally palaces to the people who occupied them. The builders of a hundred or seventy or fifty years ago built, just as we do to-day, in the very best way that was possible, having regard to the

137

materials and the labour and the knowledge available. These houses, when built, very naturally attracted large numbers of poor people living in conditions of indescribable hardship on the land.

If the serious student of this point in the problem will take the trouble to make a tour of Ireland or Brittany and get a true conception of agricultural conditions such as existed in our own country in the past, he will not wonder that the people flocked eagerly from such conditions to the far superior comfort of what are now slums.

Another false notion commonly held by the public which must be dispelled before this problem can be rightly understood is that the housing question can be answered with money. It should not be necessary to argue this point at any length after our experience of the last ten years. Since 1918, Governments and local authorities have been busy building working-class houses more or less of a pattern, and the price of the same sort of house in this short period has varied between £1,200 and £375, the fact being, as I shall show presently, that the supply of houses is a fixed quantity and that no amount of money will alter that quantity. The experience of the London County Council gives point to the argument. The cost of their housing schemes before the war was £43 per person housed. Post-war houses of pre-war design have cost £137 per person housed.

A misconception which it will be more difficult to remove from the public mind is the theory that officials help. Many an election is won by the can-

didate who will promise to strengthen the housing
department of some local authority, the idea being
that more money and more officials would produce
more houses. It is, of course, necessary that any
building effort should be under some sort of control.
There must be a standard, and the machinery must
exist for enforcing that standard. But it should be
understood that the workings or effect of all such
machinery must always be in the nature of hindrance
or restraint to building.

Ministries of Health, local authorities and housing officials are necessary evils and not, as is commonly supposed, public blessings. The man in the
street has some strange conception of a housing
official as a sort of commercial traveller pushing and
promoting the housing business, whereas, of course,
he is more in the nature of a policeman holding up
the traffic.

My personal experience of building fully confirms
this view. Twenty years ago I put up an office
building in Christopher Street, Finsbury, and was
forced by the local authorities to devote one-third
of the whole of the floor space of the building to
staircases and a system of double doors which, I believe, has now become obsolete. However that may
be, the building proved altogether useless for any
serious purpose and three or four years later I had
to abandon it at considerable loss. Within the last
few years I have erected a big building in Fleet
Street, planned by one of the foremost architects,
and have been hampered at every turn by the necessity of submitting every detail to officials, none of

whom could claim to be so well qualified as the architect who has to bow to their decisions. My building, for instance, is very superior in many respects to the standard laid down by the London Building Act, but its erection was delayed seven weeks, while I paid £70 a week ground rent, before the City and the County and the national authorities could make up their minds to give me permission to put in a much stronger foundation than the Act required. A similar experience befell me when building a workman's cottage in the country. I desired to dispense with the outside w.c., believing, surely rightly, that even a workman might be spared the necessity of going out into the rain in the middle of the night. On one occasion there were four official motor cars standing outside that half-built cottage, while the builders stood idle, and the architect, a distinguished Fellow of the Royal Institute of British Architects, wasted his time trying to convince bureaucrats that his plan could be approved without a breach of their precious regulations. A more recent experience still is in connection with Bentham Cottages, Oxted, three small houses that I put up for the use of my staff. Seeing that the Chamberlain subsidy of £70 per cottage has increased the price of cottages by £70 apiece, I felt myself to be justified in applying for the subsidy. The officials and committees concerned followed their usual leisurely procedure and after weeks of arguments and delay, gave me a licence to build with the subsidy. The licence arrived in the last week in March. It was smothered with conditions couched in official language, the first of which required that building should begin on April 1st and end on September 30th. In that case I persuaded a builder, who had been invited to tender, to dump on the site a load of bricks—which were not, as it happened, suitable for the job—on the morning of April 1st, and thus conformed for official purposes to the first requirement of the licence. When September 30th arrived the buildings were not, of course, completed, and a further application had to be made to the same officials, who were good enough to grant a further extension of time with further wordy conditions. Not only does the restraint of building by officials operate to annoy the builder, the owner and the tenant, but the ever-growing number of officials delay one another. The Lord Chief Justice, in delivering judgment in an absurd action between the King and the Minister of Health, gave a succinct illustration of this very point :

" The order was made in February ; it is now June 9th. The Ministry of Health is in London, the garden is at Hammersmith—in London ; yet between February and June they cannot discover whether this is a garden or not, and cannot save all this expense and waste of time. I recognise fully that a Government department, and you, Mr. Solicitor-General, as a Law Officer, are bound to use care to see that things are done regularly, but there is absolutely nothing in this case now except costs. It must stand over until Monday. Meanwhile, you and Mr. Montgomery can probably agree whether this is a garden, and mention it to the Court."

In December, 1920, Mr. Stephen Easten, President of the Builders' Federation, resigned his position as Director of Production in Housing at the Ministry of Health, because he could not stand the inter-departmental muddling and squabbling, the flouting of expert advice by the Ministry's own advisers, the continual contest between the Cabinet and the Minister as to which should offer the largest bribe to the Trade Unions concerned, and because of his objection to the wastefulness of the system as a whole.

By way of a third illustration, also from official evidence, the statement of the Surveyor to the Chertsey Rural Council on July 29th, 1919, may be quoted :

" We have done all we can to push matters on, and if we had had a free hand we should have had some houses ready for letting now. Instead of that we are hampered in every direction by an army of officials who are not helping but opposing housing right and left."

The Council had decided to purchase a site for twelve cottages for £225. The price was considered by the Council to be very moderate, and tenders were invited and one accepted. Everything was proceeding satisfactorily, when the District Valuer stopped the whole scheme by valuing the land at a lower figure.

Illustrations of this kind could be multiplied indefinitely, but the above are perhaps sufficient to make the simple point that officialdom may be a necessary evil but it does not promote the supply of houses.

There is another general consideration which may usefully be examined. Why should it be right or proper to house the working classes at all? Ever since the days of Lord Shaftesbury every Parliament

has passed one or more Acts to provide for the
" housing of the working classes," and the notion
has sunk deep into the public mind that something
special in the housing way should be done for those
who are known as the working classes.

Surely the absurdity of this method of thought
becomes apparent as soon as it is mentioned. It is
first of all assumed that there will, for all time, be
an individual known as the working man, who will
require a certain minimum standard down to which
it is necessary for us to build. May it not be that
this way of looking at the problem has of itself produced a good proportion of our present troubles,
and, if it continues, will surely produce much
greater trouble in the future? What, for instance, is
going to happen in twenty years' time when every
working man possesses something in the nature of a
motor-car?

All the £1,200 houses built by Dr. Addison will
be worse than useless. This way of putting the
question is not so unreasonable as it might appear
when we remember what has actually happened in
the last forty years. In 1887 Mr. George Gunton,
an American economist quoted by Sir Graham
Bower, wrote the following about housing conditions in America:

" The pest breeding and morally degrading conditions of
the homes, and the social life of the great mass of labouring
population in our industrial centres almost beggars description . . . my vocabulary is wholly inadequate to describe
the condition of the tenement houses I have seen in the
factory centres in New England."

" In a single building in the town of W———— thirty-two
feet long, twenty feet wide, three storeys high, with attics,

there habitually exist thirty-nine people of all ages. For
their use there is one pump and one privy, within twenty feet
of each other, with several sink spouts discharging upon the
ground near by."

That was in 1887, just over forty years ago, and
to-day, as we know, some twelve million American
working men have houses with garages attached, in
which they can keep the motors which they own. But
there has been no movement by Government or
by local authorities to build working-class houses in
America. They have been building houses on business principles, such as apply to every trade except
housing here, and working the market from the top
downwards, with the result that there is always a
supply of better and better houses for every grade
of society and that they are always able to go on
with the good work of pulling down the oldest and
the worst. There is no movement to build motor
cars for the working classes under government
supervision, and yet many a wage-earner owns a car
and many more use cars. Cars are built to satisfy
the demand of the market and when sold pass from
hand to hand and reach down in this way to an ever-
growing number of users. Although no motors are
being provided by Act of Parliament for the working classes, nobody can doubt that they will all have
motors long before they have houses.

All the legislation and all the official activity is
powerless to kill completely the ordinary workings
of the market, and a great deal of building of little
houses for middle-class persons is proceeding to-
day at prices ranging from £1,000 to £2,000,

houses which would, before the war, have been built from £300 to £500. In due time and season, and the quicker the better, these houses will sink to their proper money values, their owners will, in the natural course, move up to something better, and the slum-dwellers will occupy them, until in course of time they themselves get out of date and are pulled down in response to some fresh movement of the population. If, instead of worrying about the working classes at all, the building trade would build whatever the market wants, there would always be more and more houses available, and the oldest and the least desirable would drop out of the market automatically.

In considering housing and building, it should always be remembered that the building trade is a protected trade. That is why building is something of a problem all over the world. There is an almost total absence of foreign competition in connection with building. Furthermore, the restraint of transport facilities gives a new share of protection to the building industry, and the builders of Essex are not in effective competition with the builders of Norfolk. This natural protection or shelter sets a premium on laziness and dilatory methods in the building trade the world over. It accounts for the almost total absence of machinery in the building trade, for the difficulties of mass production, and has the effect of keeping the whole of the human race not only short of houses but living all the time behind what is the standard of comfort known to be possible.

10

Progress in housing comfort, due to this natural protection, is slower than progress in the supply of any other human requirement.   Seeing that this natural protection or shelter must, in the nature of things, exist, it is all the more necessary to eliminate from the building trade those forms of unnatural protection or shelter with which it is surrounded, and to promote inside the trade itself the most active competition.

There is here the possibility of a great economic experiment, an experiment which would not be popular with the building trade, but which might produce results of immense value to the rest of us. If Parliament would declare that the housing market was a free market and would make it an offence to indulge in any form of restraint in connection with the production of houses, whether by unions or combines or trade associations; if it could be enacted that everyone was free without let or hindrance to take any part that seemed to him good in the process of building, subject only to the minimum of official supervision; the whole of the problems of industry could be studied for all time from a new point of view and some very valuable information secured. It would, in my view, be quickly demonstrated that freedom would multiply indefinitely the amount of employment, would raise indefinitely the level of wages, would reduce the cost of the product, and confer much-needed benefits all round.

So much for general considerations.   The best illustration that I can give of the actual present position of the housing problem is taken from the Rural

District of Godstone. Sir William Jones and Mr.
J. Topham Brown, members of the Godstone Rural
District Council, published in February, 1926, a report of a close and detailed investigation which they
undertook, and that report is full of vital information. Godstone is a semi-rural, semi-suburban resi-
dential district twenty miles south of London. It is
predominantly Conservative in opinion, and the in-
habitants are decent, middle-class, well-to-do, sentimental folk, who have been much impressed by all
the political talk about housing since Mr. Lloyd
George promised homes for heroes.

Taking advantage of the various Acts of Parliament devised by the numerous Ministers of Health
from Dr. Addison to Mr. Chamberlain, they have
built 200 houses. The total capital expenditure of
the Council, for land and houses alone, amounts to
£272,493, or £84,594 more than the total assess-
able value of all the houses in the rural district.
Upon the completion of their present programme,
one in thirteen of the total population of the whole
district will be housed in these subsidised buildings.
The monetary loss varies according to the price of
the house from £1 per week downwards.

Here is, therefore, a case where a local authority
has taken its duties seriously, endeavoured to live
up to the best that was asked of it, and in so doing
has landed itself in serious difficulties. The present
position is : (1) A housing debt larger than the total
rateable value; (2) no provision of any kind has, or
could have, been made for depreciation, renewals,
repairs, or sinking fund; (3) as the market prices of

building become normal, the Council will be faced with the necessity of writing its property down by a figure approaching £200,000, and, having reached that stage, will not have cleared a single slum. Indeed, several houses which before the war were condemned as insanitary have been reopened to accommodate the natural growth of the population. The Council's credit is exhausted, and nothing further can be done. Meanwhile the cottage owner has been driven right off the market and the old-time popularity of an investment in bricks and mortar has been completely destroyed.

The absolute and total inability of a public authority to solve the housing problem is illustrated from the figures of the London County Council. No public body in the world has done more than the London County Council in this matter. All parties agree about this. Colonel Levita, the chairman, says :

" The magnitude of the work may be gauged by the fact that up to March 31, 1924, capital expenditure on this account amounted to no less than £15,500,000. The rent roll for the year 1924-25 is estimated at some £750,000, and accommodation for 121,000 persons has already been provided."

The London Reform Union, years ago, in pamphlet No. 3253 stated :

" More has been done under the various Housing Acts in London than in any other city—the total London expenditure under those Acts amounts, indeed, to nearly £3,000,000, or as much as that of all the rest of the United Kingdom put together."

When a politician talks of millions he always gets the public ear. The average voter is by nature in-

capable of understanding what a million is. Indeed, very few human brains can grasp the meaning
of seven figures, and the politicians' millions therefore seem to satisfy all our requirements. In reality,
however, all these official operations are merely the
echo or residue of a far larger demand and, big as
the remnants when put together appear to be, they
are seldom if ever more than a small proportion of
the natural and unregulated figure.

For instance, in the twenty-one years from 1892
to 1912 the London County Council, which had
done as much as all the rest of the United Kingdom
put together, had provided housing accommodation
for 54,141 persons. But there are 7,000,000 persons in the County of London, and had the housing
of these 7,000,000 persons been left to the most
active of the public authorities, a simple calculation
would show that it would have taken 2,800 years to
build the houses now used by those 7,000,000
persons.

There can, of course, be no objection on any
serious grounds to a public authority going into the
market, as did the London County Council in the
'nineties, to build houses for profit on commercial
lines. It may frequently happen that a public
Council may be in a better position than a private
individual to carry through a big housing scheme,
and if that scheme is devised on economic lines, if it
is made to pay, it can do no harm to any market, and
can, of course, do great good in increasing the number of houses. When, however, we reach the
present position, where local authorities are build-

ing certainly not more than a small percentage of the houses that are required, but are deliberately building at a loss and thus annihilating the rest of the market, the operations of the Council are destructive and do no good at all.

That is seen very clearly from the following announcement which appeared in *The Times* of December 13th, 1920 :

> " The Housing Committee of the London County Council has recommended the basis on which the rents shall be charged on the 582 houses that are being erected on the Roehampton estate. On an average it is estimated that the total annual outgoings per house will amount to £2 9s. 9d. per week, exclusive of rates. Of this sum 15s. 6d. a week will be paid by the tenant as rent, the balance of £1 14s. 3d. a week being met out of the public funds. The annual outgoings of each of the 90 tenements in Becket House, now being erected on the Tabard Garden estate, Southwark, are estimated at £1 11s. 1d. per week, and 12s. 2d. a week will be charged as rent, the remaining 18s. 11d. being met out of public funds."

However much credit may be given to the County Council for the provision of a house, it must be admitted that they have rendered it impossible for the persons who would normally have provided houses to carry on their operations. The figures show that things have worked that way. The highest figure ever reached by all these official activities is something over 200,000 houses a year. But we require at least that number of houses a year to provide us with one house per family per century.

After the war, the American bureaucrat got busy on the housing question, having been impressed by the example of our own Ministry of Health,

and Senator W. M. Calder was made chairman of
the Senate Committee that considered the housing
problem. In July, 1921, less than three years later,
Senator Calder was in London and gave an interview to the newspapers, in which he said :

" We discovered, after a most exhaustive survey, that the
only way to remedy a housing shortage is to leave the matter
entirely alone—no Government aid, or anything like that. It
is true that this policy caused a raising of prices in certain
parts at the time, but it had the effect of encouraging people
to build, and to-day there is no housing shortage whatever
in America. About 50 per cent of the population are house-
owners, and even the smallest new house has its garage."

A few remarks on the arithmetic of the building
trade may not seem altogether out of place here,
as it would be useful if half-a-dozen elementary
figures could be forced into the public mind. There
is a supply of building labour which for many years
has been for practical purposes fixed. The Ministry
of Labour figures show that the number of bricklayers in the three years to July, 1923-24-25, were :
56,260; 56,530; 64,260; as compared with more
than 100,000 twenty years ago. The figures for
plasterers for the same periods were : 15,760;
15,860; 17,490; and of masons : 21,880; 22,030;
23,490. *The Ministry of Labour Gazette* states that
" with the exception of carpenters and plumbers,
the number of skilled workpeople in the building
trades has varied only slightly between 1922 and
1925." These numbers are in every case much
below the figures of twenty years ago, an interesting
and startling phenomenon, for all the public and
political pressure to secure houses has actually

driven thousands of men out of the building trade. It is further known that our maximum output is in the region of 200,000 houses. Remembering that there are 9,250,000 families to be housed, making allowance for a moderate growth in population, and giving each house a life of fifty years, it will be seen that our total capacity for house building as we stand to-day is one house per family per century. This simple and startling fact explains the reason why the price of houses has fluctuated so violently in recent years. The supply is practically fixed, and the pouring of public money into a market with a fixed supply can have no other effect than to raise prices.

The astounding thing about this position is that the working classes themselves, for whom the houses are wanted, have been befooled into thinking that, in some mysterious way, their interests are threatened if any protest is raised against the monopoly of building labour. With these simple figures in front of us, it becomes evident that most of the political talk about housing schemes is utter rubbish. It may be possible by special pressure in special quarters to divert a little building effort from one class of building to another, generally a thoroughly uneconomical thing to do, but it can never be possible so to provide the houses of which politicians talk so glibly. It is not too much to say that the housing programmes of all political parties constitute a heartless fraud upon the working classes, nor can we escape the conclusion that so long as the labour monopoly is permitted to exist, the slum-dwellers must remain in the slums.

CHAPTER XIII

IT is important to emphasise that after eight or nine years, during which the entire political power of the nation, the vast financial strength of the taxpayer and the undivided force of public opinion have been behind the housing effort, the problem of housing accommodation, instead of improving, has gone from bad to worse.

In January, 1927, two different statements, each having at its back unquestioned authority, showed this to be the case. The Housing Committee of the London County Council, in its report presented on January 25th, showed that the estimated shortage of houses in Greater London, which in 1919 was 50,000, had grown by September, 1926, to 62,000, this notwithstanding the supreme effort of years to which reference has been made already and, indeed, the most successful of all the public housing efforts. On February 6th, 1927, Mr. George Hicks, Chairman of the Trades Union Congress and General Secretary of the Amalgamated Union of Building Trade Workers, in an interview with *The Westminster Gazette*, gave it as his opinion that the shortage of houses in the country had by then grown to the alarming figure of 2,000,000. How long will it take the public to realise that the politicians are robbing us of houses and making the position worse and worse?

Perhaps none of the fantastic experiments in political building has been more interesting than the attempt in 1920 and 1921 to project a building

guild.   There was a time when the Guild Socialists
seemed likely to secure control of the Socialist party.
They boasted perhaps more literary ability than any
other Socialist group, and one or two very charming
books were written explaining the delights of life
under a system of Guild Socialism.   Thanks no
doubt to the appeal of this literary effort, the
bureaucrats of 1920, encouraged by Mr. Lloyd
George, and the Trade Union officials, launched together the most perfect and complete experiment in
Guild Socialism ever attempted.   Both in Manchester and in London building guilds were formed,
and thousands of pounds of the taxpayers' money
were wasted on the salaries of doctrinaire bureaucrats, who went to absurd lengths in the making of
agreements and the concluding of arrangements
none of which, so far as I am aware, lasted for even
a couple of years.   I do not know whether there
are any Guild Socialists to-day, but the history of
the building guild movement should be more widely
known than it appears to be.   This building guild
is unlike all the many other experiments in Socialism and Communism, from the Robert Owen days
onwards, in that it had behind it the help and encouragement of no less a power than the British
Government itself.   I give the story in some detail
as told in the newspapers at the time.

" The scheme," says *The Times* of January 15th,
1920, was " received as though it were an Apoca-
lyptic vision pointing labour to a new earth "— and
the enthusiasm does not appear to have been less

complete among the officials of the Ministry of Health.

" The idea," says *The Times* in the same article, " is to set up in Manchester a Building Guild Committee representing all the building trade unions, but composed of as few members as possible. It is hoped that the membership will be limited to ten or twelve, including a representative from the administrative side and another from the technical and architectural side. The nucleus of this committee already exists, and has made a tentative offer to the Housing Committee of the city to build 2,000 houses.

" The advocates of the proposal assert that the organised workers in the industry can erect houses more quickly and more cheaply if they can establish conditions which exclude the profiteer. The Manchester City surveyor estimates that the average bricklayer will build six houses a year, but leaders of the Guild Committee assert that under their scheme a man will erect nine houses a year. The city surveyor's calculation is that the building of an artisan's house to-day will cost £940; the Guild Committee's calculation is that they could put up a better house for £800.

" They foresee no difficulty in the organisation of labour. Democratic control presents no very great problems to them. They would apply democratic principles to the appointment of all the officials, from the chief director downwards. The foremen might be appointed by the Guild Committee or by the men engaged on the particular job. They see little advantage in the one method over the other, so long as the result is the carrying on of the work with the assent and goodwill of the workers. Voluntary obedience to conditions the men themselves frame will, in the opinion of the Guild promoters, be more effective in promoting industry than reluctant obedience to capitalist authority. They also say they could set their scheme in operation in a month.

" It is proposed that the Guild should tender for and accept contracts to build artisans' houses. At this point, where the Guild begins to get in touch with established authorities, and perhaps with antagonist organisations, difficulties multiply, but the Guild advocates' final answer to them all is based on the monopoly of labour that the Guild would possess. To indicate what is in their minds, let it be imagined that the brickmakers withheld supplies of bricks. The Guild would reply by stopping all use of bricks in the area governed by the bodies constituting the Guild.

" The relations with the Housing Committee would require exact definition. One thing made quite definite is that the Guild would not enter into any financial guarantee. The building contracts would be on the lines proposed for private builders and approved organisations, the price being determined by actual cost, plus a percentage to include overhead charges and net profit. The Guild would be on the same footing as associated contractors, but it is contended that while it is right and proper that the private builder should enter into a bond, because his financial stability must be guaranteed, all that it is necessary for the Building Guild Committee to guarantee is the supply of labour. The essential thing, so the argument runs, is the building of houses. The Guild would control the labour to build them, and, having furnished proof of that control, should not be called upon to give any other guarantee. In the language of the writers on Guild Socialism, group credit, based on the power to produce, should be substituted for bank credit, based upon the purchasing power of gold.

" A further difficulty arises out of the disability of trade unions to engage in trade. It is therefore proposed that the Guilds should tender through a nominee or alternatively should assume legal powers and responsibilities as a partnership."

Less than six months later, this absurd arrangement, fantastic beyond anything that has since been tried in Moscow, was elevated to the dignity of an agreement with the British Government, and the following general statement was issued by the Minister of Health on June 6th, 1920 :

" The attitude of the Ministry of Health towards the Building Guild principle has from the start been one of sympathy; but several difficulties of detail presented themselves for solution before the Ministry could feel fully justified in approving it. The Guilds' position in reference to the purchase of materials, for example, was not clearly defined. The Co-operative Wholesale Society, however, have now agreed to give the Guilds the assistance of their extensive organisation, and it is hoped that a satisfactory arrangement may be reached.

" There was some difficulty also as to the form of remuneration to be received by the Guilds for their work. At first they adopted the proposal of remuneration by a simple percentage on the cost of the work done, not fully realising certain disadvantages of this method which are not removed by the fact that the guilds, while proposing to confer on their members the benefit of continuous employment and payment, do not intend any distribution in the nature of bonus or profit. Under such a system of simple percentage payment on cost it might easily happen, in connection with a scheme well and economically managed, that there would be an inadequate fund for this purpose; and that, in another scheme which was less carefully conducted, with consequent high costs, the fund was more than sufficient. Both results would be unsatisfactory. The Ministry desire that the amount which was to go as remuneration or extra benefit to labour should be a fixed sum per house; a plan which would secure that the benefit would be at least a little in favour of the well-managed, economical schemes.

" The portion of the percentage which, under the proposal, was allotted to cover costs of management, plant, insurance, and other overhead charges and any surplus, which by the rules of the Guild is not to be distributed in benefits, but is to be used solely to improve the plant and services of the Guild, is not subject to the same objection, and the Ministry are willing to accept a percentage basis for this for the present, though experience may show some simpler way of dealing with this also. The question of

obtaining from the Guilds some definite estimate of
costs and some suitable guarantee, so far as circumstances now permit, that the work would be carried
out to estimate, also needed settlement.

" Several conferences have recently been held
between representatives of the Guilds and officers of
the Ministry of Health with a view to arriving at a
satisfactory working basis. The promoters of the
Manchester organisation, on learning the Ministry's
views, proved quite ready to agree to certain modi-
fications of their proposals. An agreement has now
been reached, and it is of importance as illustrating
principles which may prove capable of more extended application.

" The Guild have agreed to give a definite estimate of cost for each type of house. This estimate
must be regarded as reasonable by both the parties
concerned—the Guild and the local authority—and
must be approved by the Ministry. The Guild's remuneration will be by a lump sum of £40 per house
—to provide for a full-time week (regardless of
weather) for those employed on the contract and for
other purposes of the Guild. A further allowance
of 6 per cent. on the prime cost of the house will be
made to cover the cost of plant and other overhead
charges, such as salaries of buyers, supervisors and
others who are not wholly employed on the building
site.

" In the event of the actual cost of a house prov-
ing less than the estimated cost, the actual cost only,
plus the £40 and the 6 per cent. overhead charges,
will be paid by the local authority. The Guild

recognise and agree that in any case the 6 per cent. for overhead charges should not be paid on any increase in the cost of materials taking place during the progress of the work, although for the purpose of determining whether the estimate has been exceeded or not, fluctuations in the standard rates of labour and prices of materials will be allowed for.

" If the actual cost should prove to be more than the estimated cost, after the usual allowance for the fluctuation in wages, rates and prices, the Guild will receive the £40 as above, but the 6 per cent. will not be payable on the amount of the extra cost.

" The agreement provides also that the Co-operative Wholesale Society may be associated in the contract for the purchase of materials. The contract must include a break clause allowing the contract to be broken after three months if the costs should exceed the estimate by more than any increase that has occurred in the meantime in the rates of wages and in the standard cost of materials. The Co-operative Wholesale Society, on being satisfied with the contract, will insure the local authority against loss under the contract for an insurance premium of one-eighth per cent., 2s. 6d. per £100. The Guild are in agreement with the Ministry that a proper costing system shall be adopted."

Exactly ten days later, on June 16th, 1920, the London Building Guild announced that it was in being. Its ambitious scheme to build houses for London and, indeed, for the nation, on the Guild principle, was outlined in a pamphlet issued by the

National Federation of Building Trades Operatives. This pamphlet explained that : " The first and immediate duty of the Guild is to mobilise the necessary labour to build the houses so urgently needed by the nation, and to build them in the best possible manner at the lowest possible cost."

The constitution of the Guild set out its objects, the first three of which were (1) To carry on the industry of builders, decorators and general contractors; (2) To undertake all branches of supply, whether as merchant, manufacturer, or transporter; (3) To carry on any other work which the Society may think necessary or desirable in connection with the above objects.

It is important to notice that apart from all the building trade unions and the Ministry of Health, the Guild scheme was backed by the wealth of the Co-operative Wholesale Society, thus removing any question of inability to succeed through lack of finance.

A few days after the conclusion of the agreement with the Ministry, *The Times* announced that " a housing contract for some hundreds of thousands of pounds has been given to the newly-formed London Builders' Guild by one of the Metropolitan local authorities, and negotiations are proceeding with a view to contracts of a similar character in the near future."

Within eighteen months the guild idea had exploded. The trade unions declined to find a penny to support it. Labour fell away, the C.W.S. withdrew, and what remained of the organisation was ignominiously sold to a private contractor. The Labour Publishing Co., in 1923, published *The Builders' History*, by R. W. Postgate, which tells the dismal story in detail.

Similarly, at the height of the building guild enthusiasm, the furniture workers were smitten with the same ideas and ideals and a furniture guild was established in September, 1921. It went into bankruptcy eighteen months later, in March, 1923. I mention this minor example because the making of furniture is a much simpler process than the making of houses. It not only requires less money, but it is not so involved in complications such as land and legislation. It is therefore valuable to know that the guild idea, tried in two distinct fields, differing as widely as houses and furniture, having behind it in each case the support of the trade unions at the very height of their power and, further, having in each case the friendly co-operation of the Government, ended in complete fiasco in less than a couple of years.

The politician never profits by experience, never learns from failure. The 1920-21 building guild experiment did not differ in essentials from many similar experiments in Communism. It had, indeed, the advantage of a previous experiment in building when, inspired by Robert Owen, the Operative Builders' Union in 1833 formed a guild in Birmingham. Birmingham, however, even in those early days, did better than Manchester or London, in that the guild did at least build a "guild-hall" for itself, whereas the same social movement of the twentieth century leaves no traces of its activities behind it.

While the trade unions, the Socialists and the Government departments were willing to put all their energy and influence into a fantastic scheme for establishing industry upon a basis of Communism, none of these great public forces have been willing to give any real support or have shown any reasonable interest in schemes for alternative methods of building. Wooden houses, concrete houses and steel houses, to say nothing of numerous minor experiments in pressed earth and breeze blocks, have all failed to receive encouragement, to put the matter quite mildly. Several serious attempts at mass production have been rendered abortive, generally by trade union action, but more frequently by national stupidity. There have been schemes for importing wooden houses complete, but these were not likely to succeed in a market where even the importation of wooden doors and window frames is practically stopped by the close combination of masters and men. There are a few cases, but very few, where these difficulties have been overcome. Sir Tudor Walters, working quietly in the South Yorkshire coalfield, has built thousands of cottages in model villages, described in his book *The Building of Ten Thousand Houses*, on lines that might well have been adopted all over the country.

We have seen that the building trade furnishes perhaps our best example of the folly of a policy of restriction. By a study of its history one can see how one restriction leads to another and in the end to the disappearance of liberty itself. Our housing troubles began with the early Housing Acts as long as seventy years ago. Those Acts have led to some hundreds of amending Acts, every one of them purporting to " house the working classes." Restrictions upon building by legislation lead easily and naturally to restrictions upon building labour by trade unions. The next step, even easier—for every slippery slope becomes easier the further we descend —is the formation of trade rings. Having a market limited by legislation and a capacity limited by union restrictions, it becomes almost a necessity for the suppliers of materials to make arrangements for the regulation and limitation of their contributions to the scheme. All this failing to act, we now have joint councils and are threatened with an extension of the idea of joint responsibility. Responsibility is perhaps hardly the word, for none of these monopolists are in practice responsible to the rest of us who want the houses. The result of it all is a dwindling industry with an ever-growing shortage. This condition of affairs will remain as long as the public rests under the impression that houses can be built with votes, and forgets that the attempts at Socialism which have actually been made in our own time have inevitably failed to produce the goods.

CHAPTER XIV

AT this point in our discussion of the housing situation, a word of caution must be uttered on the question of figures. Any student of the housing problem will be struck by the considerable differences that are disclosed even by official figures. All the many reports available are at variance, and the most contradictory conclusions can be drawn from the figures issued by different parties and at different times. It must be remembered that we have had three distinct official policies in connection with building—Mr. Lloyd George and Dr. Addison with the Coalition Government and millions of housing bonds; Mr. Bonar Law, and later Mr. Baldwin, with what is strangely called a Conservative policy; and in between Mr. Ramsay MacDonald and Mr. Wheatley with a new heaven and a new earth. Each of these parties has to justify its existence by showing the other two to be wrong, and each of them produces figures in pursuance of that amiable object. These figures, when examined, are found to differ in no essential way from the figures which issue in such impressive volume from Moscow. The great majority of them are concerned with the estimates of various committees and so-called authorities as to what is wanted, what should be, or what various innumerable schemes are calculated to produce. I often think that if the public would give up its interest in citizenship and sociology and turn its mind to arithmetic and statistics, the world would be a very great deal more comfortable. It is not necessary to argue with the business man on the unreliability of figures and the pitfalls they represent. The Bankruptcy Courts are kept busy and thrive on the general ignorance of these subjects.

There is another danger about official figures. Even if true they are generally misleading and, as I have remarked before, if you mention the mere word million to the average elector he is satisfied. But it often happens that the millions figuring so largely in official statistics are mere drops in the ocean of private and individual activity that they endeavour to dam up. During the war, for instance, there was an attempt to control paper, and Mr. Hall Caine, jnr., was given the position of Controller, I suppose because his father had put more ink on to more paper than any other living man. But the spectacle of young Hall Caine controlling paper was the most ludicrous of all the absurd spectacles associated with the political mania of control. He produced the usual figures with the usual millions, but he overlooked the fact (and so did those who were engaged at that time in controlling everything) that every day of every week in this little island alone there are sixty million transactions between individuals involving the sale and purchase of paper, and that no official machinery can ever do anything but reduce that tremendous volume of activity. During the war it may have been desirable to reduce activity, although that remains a question of doubt, but no doubt can exist of the necessity for the opposite policy in time of peace.

There is a point here in connexion with housing that is very seldom made, but that I think needs to be stressed. Almost all our other industries are under a normal obligation, which they readily accept, to keep in stock a surplus of their products, which they hold at the disposal of the rest of us. The tailoring trade or the furniture trade does not deny its natural obligation to make its product, put it upon the shelves of the shop or into the warehouse and then wait for the buyer to inspect and purchase at his leisure. Production in all the free industries is ahead of consumption, and thus it comes about that we are well supplied with all those commodities where the network of control and restriction is not so closely woven.

The building trade, however, has been legislated and organised into a position where production is always behind consumption and where, if at any time there is the merest sign of a surplus of production, something is supposed to be wrong. I fail to see why there should not always be a surplus of houses. A healthy building trade, like any other healthy trade, would always have a proportion of its products on its hands, and the consumer, or user, of houses would always have an option or a choice. Thus, as with every other trade, the bad, the expensive and the inefficient would be constantly disappearing from the market and a process of replacement from bad to good and from good to better would always be proceeding. There is no reason in theory why we should not rebuild England every fifty years, and if that were done the standard of

living would be always improving and many times
the number of builders would be always busy. Such
an ideal could be realised if we would only understand that the aim and object of industry is to deliver
the goods; and if we would give up our present way
of looking at these problems, which can be expressed in a sentence—" Wages without work and
to hell with the consumer."

The most superficial examination of our methods
of production, of the market or of the habits of the
consumer in almost any other trade, will show that
we do, in fact, develop on these lines when we have
the blessings of freedom, competition and private
enterprise and when we are actuated by the common-
sense ideals of service.

The science of political economy or, as it is now
called, economics, still talks of supply and demand,
and there is very sound wisdom behind the order in
which the founders of the science placed these two
words. The building trade is working upon the unsound theory of demand and supply and hence there
is trouble. All the national schemes for building
are founded upon the idea that by ascertaining beforehand what is the demand, better arrangements
can be made to supply it. That theory I believe to
be unsound. Supply must precede demand in any
healthy condition of things. There may be a prospective demand, a demand which the supplier be-
lieves will be forthcoming when the supply is ready,
but in normal, ordinary, economic business supply
must come before demand.

The truth of this is very clearly demonstrated in

the auction room. The auctioneer produces the supply and says : " Here is a house ; what will you bid for it? " One has only to put this question the other way round to see the absurdity of the position into which we have allowed ourselves to drift. Imagine, for instance, an auctioneer saying, " If I presently produce a house, what will you bid for it? "—and then asking for bids without offering any guarantee that the house will be produced. Having secured his bids the auctioneer would go back to the builder, who would then become the supreme master of the situation and who would say that he would think it over, with the result that a few days later he would return with a demand for a higher price. That is almost exactly what is happening in the housing market to-day. The politicians are endeavouring to reverse the natural position, to make " supply and demand " read " demand and supply," and to place the producer in a superior position to the consumer—a damaging and unnatural operation which, as I have previously emphasised, never has worked and never will.

No question of national importance has been so constantly and so prominently in the public eye during recent years as this problem of housing. No question has been so woefully mismanaged and so hopelessly tangled, thanks to the intervention of the politicians in a matter which is essentially one for the business man and private enterprise. All parties have been equally guilty of spreading the notion that houses can be built by votes, that the tens of thousands of people who want houses badly had only to vote for this party or the other and houses would spring up like mushrooms, so that the wants of the masses would be satisfied.

To help to understand this housing blunder thoroughly one has only to apply the modern ideas on housing to one's own business. The housing question has become so enveloped in an almost impenetrable political fog that it is difficult to discuss it in simple terms. If one substitutes for houses some other article, say books, one sees more clearly the folly of it all. I select books because, as a publisher, I know something about them. My present position is that I have to go out into the market, take off my hat to my customer, inquire after his health and express the hope that he will honour me with his esteemed commands. I have to submit to his criticism of the books which I produce and have to make my terms agreeable in every way to him. Chastened by this experience of the road, I go back to my office, where I find a small army of persons associated with the production of books—paper makers, writers, printers, binders, block makers and the rest—and, having my customer's views fresh in my mind, am able to impress these persons with the need for economy and efficiency. In this way satisfactory books are produced and business is maintained and the book market is supplied.

Now imagine that the politicians were to raise the cry—the very sensible cry from my point of view as a publisher—that everybody must have books, that it is our right as citizens to enjoy good literature, that every Englishman should have his share of books and so on; and supposing we all voted for books. Instantly my frame of mind, and the frame of mind of everyone connected with the production of books, would undergo a change. Instead of having to go into the market with my hat off, seeking orders and making my price satisfactory to the buyer, I should find buyers ranged up in a queue outside my office, each one furnished with the appropriate official chit entitling him to books, and the result of a Government-backed demand of this kind on the matter of supply and on the matter of price can readily be imagined.

If everyone would apply this test to his own particular line of business there would be a clearer and sounder general view of the reasons why we are not likely to get houses by voting for them. If in regard to housing there had been, in the post-war period, the same free play for private enterprise as there has been allowed to the book market, we should not to-day be suffering so acutely from housing embarrassments and the numerous evils that are a direct consequence of the lamentable lack of dwellings.

CHAPTER XV

COMBINES AND PROFITS

No single term in the English language has been responsible for more political folly than the word combine, and very few words are less well understood.

What should be the attitude of the Individualist to trusts and combines, and all those reorganisations and amalgamations which are so popular in industry to-day? That question brings out rather sharply the disadvantages of the word "Individualism" as indicating a philosophy or an economic point of view. The word suggests a single individual, and lays us open to the charge that we stand for the discredited doctrine of every man for himself and the Devil take the hindmost. Individualism does sound as if we mean that every single person should be an independent unit, and that any form of combination or collective action is to be deprecated.

The attitude of the Socialists towards trusts and combines is, as might be expected, illogical and double-faced. They try to get the best of both worlds and make use of combines to support arguments in favour of two opposite conclusions. On the one hand, they will wax eloquent against combinations of capitalists who through money-power force their will on the community and serve their own sordid ends. On the other hand, they are frequently found arguing, and this is perhaps at the moment the more popular Socialist line, that as industry is developing into big units the State should proceed to continue that heaven-sent process and put the whole of industry into big groups controlled by the State, instead of by financiers.

As so often happens in these big public questions, we are left without any agreed definition of terms, and I have yet to discover what we generally mean when we use the word " combine," or what is conveyed by the term " trust." In our loose conversation we use both these words to describe any big concern without bothering to notice that bigness may serve to mark totally different characteristics. We talk of the tobacco combine, and everyone will admit that the Post Office is a trust, and yet there is practically no shred of similarity in the organisation, the practice, the fabric or the construction of these two great institutions.

The Post Office is both a combine and a trust. It contains all the powers and all the evils of a monopoly, and in addition all the powers which are showered upon it by the legislature, and which are not, of course, available for use by the ordinary financial or economic combine. The Post Office gives exactly what service it likes, it dictates its own prices, and, furthermore, it forbids others to offer any competition, and, worst of all, it is completely and absolutely independent of the necessity to make a profit. It does happen to make a profit in some of its departments, but there is nothing in its constitution which imposes upon it the necessity to do anything of the kind. There is within it no inherent obligation to give satisfaction to its customers, and with its Parliamentary backing it is able to extort revenues in respect of work which it never performs.

The best illustration of this is the number of letters which, for rapid expedition, are sent through the railway companies, and which have by law to bear Post Office stamps, although the Post Office never sees them. We can freely admit, without in any way impairing our argument, that notwithstanding all these theoretical blemishes the Post Office does work well on the whole. It may be that as there is no alternative we have accustomed ourselves to Post Office methods, just as perforce we have to accustom ourselves to the English climate; there is nothing else that we can do, and nobody seriously suggests that the service of the Post Office should be undertaken by private enterprise.

In considering the Post Office it should not be overlooked that the work it does is not analogous to the work of an industry. A good many people go off the rails on this simple point. The Post Office is correctly described as a public utility institution. It produces nothing, it manufactures nothing, it delivers no tangible values in the service which it renders; it is, in fact, a distributing service and not a trade. To understand the difference between a public institution like this and an individualistic trading enterprise, whatever its size and however completely it fills its field, it is only necessary to take a simple example.

Suppose, for instance, that a great and powerful institution like *The Daily Telegraph* were put into the position and given the status and the backing of the Post Office, things would be so arranged that nobody would be allowed to know the bank rate or the price of Consols, except through the pages of *The Daily Telegraph*. It would be ordered that admission to a theatre was only possible on presentation of the coupon taken out of the Drama Page in the same newspaper. It would be an offence to read the Prime Minister's speech without first paying twopence to the proprietors of *The Daily Telegraph*, whether you read the speech in that paper or not. These far-fetched suggestions, in every way comparable to the conditions under which the Post Office works, demonstrate the stupidity of quoting the latter as an illustration of what industry might be. I cannot conceive of the most bigoted Socialist holding up any newspaper in such conditions as a model of industrial enterprise.

Individualism and Collectivism in industry are not questions of size. The largest undertaking can be individualistic and quite a small undertaking can be Collectivist in character. The difference, indeed, is entirely a question of the principles on which the undertaking is constructed, and those principles are seen most clearly if we study the undertaking in its relation to the customers or the consumers. In the case of the Post Office the consumer is tied hand and foot. He has no opportunity to avail himself of any alternative, no choice, no preference, no option of any sort, kind, or description.

Perhaps the most wonderful example of Individualist effort in the world is an institution quite as large as our own Post Office—the Meat Trust of Chicago.   The Chicago meat packer is not an illustration of the blessings of Individualism and freedom which will make any wide appeal to any section of the British public, but for that reason it is perhaps all the better as an example, because nobody in this country at least can be suspected of any personal bias or prejudice on behalf of this particular foreign institution.

The Meat Trust of Chicago shows how organisation and amalgamation and big finance can be made to work to the benefit of the whole human race.   It is to the operations of these people that we owe our habits as a meat-eating people.   There was a time, even in England with all its luxuriant pasture and with a very small population, when the bulk of us only had a mouthful of meat to celebrate a birthday, or at best on Sundays.   The labouring classes of three generations ago had to perform their strenuous duty without the assistance of the nourishment which they now derive from plentiful supplies of meat.

But the Meat Trust is no monopoly, and can never be anything in the nature of a monopoly. The marvellous achievements of the Chicago pork packer have been made in competition with every cottager and every farmer in the whole world.   Any reader who has experience of pig-keeping will confirm this fact.   When we consider that the pig in Kent or Essex may be fed for almost nothing on the refuse of the house or garden, and that even so bacon from that pig cannot be marketed in the village where it lived at as low a price as prime bacon which has travelled all the way from Chicago, the marvels of the Meat Trust cannot fail to win our admiration and, indeed, our thanks.

The truth is, of course, that the meat people, in competition with the whole world, actually sell meat at less than the cost of production, and by the application of science and machinery and organisation to the business on a big scale are able to turn their losses into huge profits by the skilful marketing of by-products, which can only be retrieved owing to their large-scale operations. It used to be said that the stock yards of Chicago used up everything about a pig except its squeak, but it is doubtful whether that is not now an under-statement. I understand that the intestines of even the pig have been brought to the service of the musical-instrument trade, and it helps me to understand the technicalities of the popular jazz when I consider that its economic basis may be the squeak which had hitherto escaped the capabilities of the pork packers !

Some people get on their hind legs and talk wildly about combines as soon as they see a profit which runs into any figures worth mentioning. These are the people who accept the Marxian falsehood, and believe that the price of an article is the "cost plus the profit," a folly all too prevalent amongst us. Most of the big profits which form the subject of speeches on the iniquity of trusts and combines are quite definitely profits made out of economy, as shown in the case of the meat trade. Indeed, the best definition of profit that I know, and

12

the one that most correctly describes those big profits which are the subject of so much criticism, is "commission on economy."

The ignorance of the general public on this question of profit is one of those fundamental troubles which make it so hard to get sane economic arrangements into public affairs. An indolent industry full of old-fashioned, lazy, out of date people may make a 20 per cent. profit on its turnover, using its capital only once in two years, and thus disclose a profit or dividend of 10 per cent. upon its shares. Such an industry, although it may be robbing the public, will pass without comment or criticism and will never be the subject of any abuse. Alongside there may be an enterprising industry which with push and go is content to take a 5 per cent. profit on its turnover, but uses its capital five times in the course of the year, and thus discloses a 25 per cent. dividend on the capital invested. The consumer is, of course, infinitely better off in the latter case than in the former, and yet the 25 per cent. will be sure to bring howls of indignation and long stories about trusts and combines.

No question is more in need of study and debate than this one of profits. The word itself has come to be regarded as having an immoral meaning, the profiteer is quite definitely a criminal, and the maker of any sort of profit is looked upon as a doubtful character. It is important to notice that this state of mind is peculiarly English. Dislike of profits and limitation of output, "ca' canny," are two of our own economic specialities neither of which is to

be found to so serious an extent elsewhere. There
is something about a profit which seems to cause us
a peculiar mental irritation. If we talk of beef, we
seldom mention quantity or quality, we are not interested in its uses or its influence on human life
and health, we know little about it and care less.
But the mere mention of beef to any dozen Englishmen or women will be certain to lead straight to a
violent railing against the beef packers' profits. If
soap is talked about at all, nobody bothers to discuss the advantage which this generation enjoys in
having twice as much soap as its fathers had, but
the conversation is sure to produce an expression of
dissatisfaction at Lever's millions. This ingrained
antipathy to profits goes right through society and
is perhaps most noticeable where it should least be
expected.

Of what is profit composed? How does it arise?
Where does it come from? If analyzed, it will be
seen to consist of three ingredients: (1) the earnings
of management, (2) interest on capital, (3) an insurance premium for the risk undertaken. Now
each of these ingredients is accepted without question in every walk of life: nobody suggests that any
one of them is immoral, yet when they are lumped
together and called profit, we are asked to believe
that they constitute an evil which is responsible for
the ills with which Society is afflicted, and that in
the new world which the doctrinaires will create,
profit will find no place.

We human beings are funny creatures; we are
liable to feel a certain irritation at the thought of

another making a profit out of us. We must have
our little grumble or else we do not really enjoy
ourselves; but to turn that feeling into a great
political movement may be, and is, a very dangerous thing to do.

Profits can be made in two ways, either by adding
to the selling price or by reducing the costs of production. Additions to the selling price can only be
made when there is scarcity, and the present habit
of the world in the direction of developing scarcity,
limiting production and restricting exchange is
creating innumerable opportunities for profiteers to
add to prices. Every act which tends to discourage
production by anybody swells profits. It is
pathetic to the student of these matters to see the
labouring classes deceived, by people who ought to
know better, into believing that they can improve
wages by limiting production. Exactly the reverse
is the case; but it is the fact that every such limitation adds to the chances of profit. Profits in the
bulk—the best profits, normal profits, and the
profits of times of prosperity—are made by reducing
costs, a process which, once begun, generally improves money wages and always improves "real"
wages. The whole tribe of economists, from the
earliest times, have never been able to suggest an
alternative to profits as a cost reducer.   Profit is
really the cheapest thing we have; it is the most
powerful agent for economy that we yet know.

Industry exists to supply the goods; there is no
other reason or excuse for it. The test of a good

industry is a very simple one.   Does it do four simple things:

1. Pay adequate wages.
2. Produce maximum quantities of appropriate quality.
3. Charge minimum prices.
4. Produce enough profit to tempt more capital into the business.

An individualistic industry established on an independent, free, and competitive basis, if successful, always stands this test, and it does not matter whether it is a combine or a trust, or even a monopoly, if those four conditions are respected. There is no advantage to the public in having a lot of little people making a given article if one big concern can make that article more economically; but we can never know, never be sure, that that condition is fulfilled unless there is all the time complete and absolute liberty for the little man to start up on his own in competition.

An individualistic enterprise, as distinguished from a socialist institution like the Post Office, is subject to two oppressive and exacting conditions which, if allowed to remain, must keep the enterprise healthy and useful.   The first condition is that every penny which goes into its coffers is freely provided by consumers who have no compulsion upon them to use the commodity or product, and the other and complementary condition is that the consumers are free to go elsewhere, and other producers are free to enter the market.   None of these conditions applies to the Post Office; none of them would be applied to a nationalised mining industry, and not one of them is compatible with the theory of Socialism.

A good deal of misapprehension exists on the question of size. It is far too commonly assumed that if only an institution can be big it must be good, and thus there are a number of words freely used to-day which are regarded by some people as almost sacred and always helpful. Such words are " organise," " co-ordinate," " amalgamate " and " co-operate." It does become necessary, therefore, to enter a caveat against this loose assumption to which so many people jump so readily.

There is a very definite limit in every industry to the advantages secured from size. That limit varies from industry to industry. I can well believe that with simple commodities like soap or cotton it is possible to go on adding to the size of a business without impairing its efficiency, and without adding to its cost. But that is not true when more complicated trades are considered, such, for instance, as engineering, or printing, or ship-building. In each of these cases the product is so varied, the conditions are so complicated, the application of personal skill to detail is so essential, that there is a very definite limit beyond which size becomes an extravagance and not an economy.

Size, in the hands of the professional bureaucrat, is, as we have seen in some previous chapters, a definite danger and a heavy expense. Big business is bad enough in its tendency to develop red tape, but to the bureaucratic method red tape is essential. In big business it is possible to allow to individuals the liberty to act upon their own, to make mistakes and occasionally to act in defiance of the principles which govern the concern as a whole, but such liberty can never be given to bureaucrats or to Government institutions. Public money and public affairs must always be conducted with such strict regard for rule and regulation, principle and order as to incur inevitably enormous expense and inordinate delay.

If our needs were supplied by a number of individualistic combinations it would at least be possible for the boot trade to work with a single eye to the efficient production of boots, and the coal trade to work with the sole aim of producing coal in the most convenient manner, but the moment that these institutions are brought under public or Government control then they must perforce work to the rules and regulations and observe the obligations which are common to public affairs. In this way alone vast additions are made to the cost of anything which comes under the hand of the bureaucrat, and in this way alone it can be shown that the Government could never provide, at any cost which any people could pay, sufficient quantities of commodities to keep us in a state of civilisation.

The real test, therefore, of an industry or service, the real difference between a Collectivist institution and the Individualist method, is to be found by applying the twin tests of service and freedom. If the industry is dependent for its well-being, and the well-being and comfort of all who work in it, upon the good opinion of the consumers, then it is a sound

Individualist industry. If there is complete freedom for anybody to enter the market on the one hand, or for any consumer to leave it on the other, then it does not matter how big is the combine which is operating in the market, or how small is the unit of production. If the producer is under an obligation to serve and the market is free, there is no question at all of combines or trusts, as those words are commonly used.

CHAPTER XVI

CONTROL AND LIBERTY

WHILE we all want liberty, we are all subject to control, whether it be the control of natural forces or some artificial control under which we have allowed ourselves to come.

The ambition to command, to order, to boss, to control is a very laudable ambition and is part of the nature of that large minority who are really responsible for keeping things going and making life interesting for the rest. It does not follow that everyone who wants to command is capable of doing so, nor does it follow that at any given time those in command are the ideal persons for the job. It is, however, very important that students of economics, sociology and politics should give the closest study to the problem of command, and strive to discover the system or the social arrangement which will ensure that the power to command tends to concentrate into the hands of those who have passed some test of ability and shown themselves to possess some of the necessary qualifications.

There is nothing wrong about the desire to boss or to control, although it is generally accompanied by a certain amount of conceit, but a good strong character requires a modicum of conceit, just as a good savoury needs a sprinkling of pepper. A certain amount of greediness is essential to the making of a good appetite, and, as long as the greediness is thoroughly subordinated to other considerations, no objection can properly be taken to it.

Most of us believe that we can do some things

rather better than the other fellow. It may be true or untrue, but that makes no difference and does not alter our belief. Either the husband or the wife in every married pair looks upon the other as utterly devoid of wisdom and common-sense in the matter of poking the fire; or how many women are there who are satisfied with the skill of other women in the matter of holding a baby? Similarly, every good office boy has his own plans for improving the business when the present head has gone to his funeral or disappeared in some other way. Underneath the actions and thoughts of most of us is the very laudable and proper desire to command, or desire to have the opportunity of doing things in some other, and as we think, better way. There is thus constituted a big natural check upon the indiscretions of those who possess responsibility and a big natural source from which vacancies in command can always be filled.

There are great dangers in command. That, again, is a natural thing, which will remain with us whatever economic or political system we devise. No Act of Parliament, no political arrangement, can put into the brains of those at the top the exact amount of wisdom that is required at any given time and in any given circumstances. History is full of the mistakes of bad bosses from Pharaohs to Kaisers.

Indeed, there would be very little interest in history apart from these mistakes. The people who succeed in getting along for a generation or two without blunders in high quarters have a very good time while they live, but make no mark in history, and leave no material for the historian.

The most dangerous and objectionable sort of command is that which relies upon force. All who dominated and ruled the ancients and the barbarians maintained their position by virtue of their personal strength or because of the strength of the army or the party which adhered to them. Command which relies upon force is quite irresponsible and as we now know, or as we imagine ourselves to know, is altogether objectionable.

It is only in the last couple of centuries that modern civilisation has developed the ideal way of selecting rulers, commanders, chiefs and bosses. Notwithstanding all the criticism that is day by day levelled against the capitalist system, it is undoubtedly true that capitalism does, on the whole, provide industry and commerce with the best people that are available at any moment for the purpose of leading and bossing. The capitalist boss is, with few exceptions, entirely free from the objection to which the older boss was liable, the objection of having force at the back of him. It is, of course, true that here and there, now and again, some millionaire or combination of moneyed people will, for a brief spell, get such a command of some market as to give them all the advantages of force and power; but most of my readers will not make the mistake of confounding the antics of some multi-millionaire with the workings of the capitalist system, which comprises every little shopkeeper and every little maker of anything the world over.

Under capitalism, or as I prefer to call it Individualism, a man can only secure control of some industrial enterprise by giving satisfaction to others, and can only hold that control so long as he continues to give that satisfaction. He is under the strict necessity of satisfying his customers all the time and, were it not for the false labour position created by the politicians, he would be under the same necessity all the time of giving like satisfaction to those who work for him. The American business man certainly has to give every bit as much thought to satisfying his workers as he does to satisfying his customers.

Capitalism has another advantage over the old-fashioned way of selecting controllers on account of their strength or their ability to enlist force in their service. Instead of revolutions and assassinations, which were at one time the only means through which a change of control could be secured, capitalism has a bankruptcy court, and every year 8,000 capitalist bosses are put down from their seats because they have failed to give that satisfaction to others which alone could qualify them to remain in the market. Their property, their machinery and their trade have passed over to others, and so the business of governing material things is constantly passing from the hands of the incompetent.

It is thus easy to see that Socialism, in its theory that it will substitute other schemes for the market or the money test, is really an endeavour to get back to the irresponsibility and the dangers of force. No Socialist has ever yet ventured an opinion as to what is to happen under this precious system to the man who, having been put into a position of command, proves unworthy of that position. This is really one of the biggest difficulties that we all have to face, and a difficulty which has never yet been faced by any Socialist writer. Most of us can call to mind some acquaintance of ours who is in a position of command and who is quite unfitted to hold that position. It may be some young man who has succeeded to a business built up by his father, or it may be some engineer or surveyor or clerk in the employment of a public authority. In both cases the work done to the order of these people is unsatisfactory work, and the public loses some advantage which it would possess if sensible and suitable people were in these posts.

But then the personal difficulty arises. In our civilised state we don't call a man a fool even when we believe him to be one; we just leave him alone; we hope he may improve, and in any case we decide that a quiet life is better than a quarrel with a neighbour. Thus it comes about that the fool in the public service or the fool in a Socialised industry is almost entirely safe. The worst that can happen to him is that his superiors will look out for an opportunity of moving him on to some other department so that he can practise his foolery without inconvenience to themselves. It is common knowledge that when some new Government department is opened every other Government department always showers upon it generous offers of help from people with whom they desire to dispense.

But the son of a wealthy father in charge of a business, and incapable of controlling it, is in a very different position. Nobody says a word to him; nobody tells him he is a fool, but his customers quietly leave him. Two things, in fact, happen. Others more capable of commanding take his trade away, and he goes into the bankruptcy court. The process is automatic, regular and never fails. It provides the rest of us, the consumers, with the guarantee that all the time we have in charge of those services on which we depend for our material needs the best brains that are available to render them.

The mixing up of politics and industry, now such a very popular game, involves us in the necessity of sorting out afresh those questions which are really political questions and separating them from those other matters which are economic problems. Politics is, of course, a game of force. The politicians are always able to enlist and use the force of the nation to carry through the decisions which they take; that must be so.

The old-fashioned despot was able himself to decide in which direction the force of the nation should be used. Now, with the blessing of democracy, the nation can take that decision for itself, but, as we have seen in previous chapters, the decision being taken, the nation must exercise its authority or carry out its wish through the hands of bureaucrats. As some of the leading judicial authorities quite recently pointed out, one of the big mistakes at the moment is the modern habit of passing over to bureaucrats not only the power to put a decision into operation, but the power to take the decision itself.

That habit of giving power to bureaucrats is most noticeable in those cases where politicians have seen fit to trespass into the realm of industry, production and economics. It is the more dangerous because, as we have seen above, there is not a shred of a safeguard in the shape of any test by which we can know whether the bureaucrat is giving satisfaction or not.

The bankruptcy test which keeps the field of business clear of the worst of the weeds of inefficiency imposes upon the business man the necessity of knowing a great deal about his business. Every business, however simple it may seem upon the surface to be, is full of intricate complications, technical and abstruse difficulties, and very few businesses are so easy as to require much less than a lifetime thoroughly to understand them. From the way some people talk it would seem as if any business could be run by anybody who has a bank account and the ability to smoke a cigar. I listened the other day to one of the most interesting twenty-minute speeches that I remember from a man in the herring fishing trade. He told us how his father and his grandfather before him had devoted their lives to the problems associated with the simple herring, gave us some insight into the improvements that he was making and left me with the impression that three generations of close application and study were not sufficient to understand all there is to know about so simple a commodity and so simple a trade.

And yet the politician or the bureaucrat will almost always profess to tell us everything there is to know about every trade there is. This is, of course, the leading characteristic of the Socialist politician. Take six names representing all the different sections of the Labour party: Oswald Mosley, Jack Jones, Saklatvala, Kenworthy, Lansbury and Maxton. Any one of these six will presume to tell you, if you ask him, with certainty and confidence exactly what to do with coal, rubber, cotton, arms, taxes, health, employment, prayer books, currency and housing. It is almost certain that every one of the six has made many speeches on every one of these complicated questions, and it is absolutely certain that any one of the six would, if given the chance, accept complete responsibility with full powers for controlling and arranging any of these matters and proceed to boss the rest of us without any check or safeguard or test of knowledge, efficiency, or capability.

It is, in my judgment, a physical impossibility, within the space of one human life and with the limitations of one human brain, to know more than a fractional percentage of the knowledge required to grasp the ten or eleven problems that I have mentioned. If these matters are left under Individualism to be handled by persons who, in the competition of the market, will have to demonstrate their fitness to handle them, many little difficulties will arise by the way, but on the whole, and in the end, the public will receive the best service. If, on the other hand, these questions are to be put into the political machine to be settled by blatant ignoramuses and to be subject to their control backed by political force, all hope of progress disappears, and the certainty of decay takes its place.

It is surprising to me how even a patient public like our own tolerates the impertinence of politicians who claim to know so much and to be so clever. It is only in politics, and especially in Socialism, that one gets this bumptious and pretentious ignorance. Outside the realm of politics men of position make no such claims to skill and wisdom. No one, for instance, has ever heard Sir Oliver Lodge on Currency, Mr. St. John Ervine on Cotton Problems, Sir William Orpen on the Prayer Book, the Governor of the Bank of England on Health, Mr. Charles Chaplin on Coal, or Miss Sybil Thorndike on Rubber, and yet all these people are as well qualified to express opinions on these questions as Mr. Oswald Mosley or Mr. Wheatley. Every one of these persons I have named will go down to history for some definite contribution to human thought and progress, and will be known to generations which will never hear of our current politicians.

Politics may be defined as "the application of force to the expressed will of the nation," a definition which rules out politics as an agency through which any of our material needs can be supplied, because, as we have seen, force cannot give us those safeguards and those guarantees of proficiency which can only be secured through competition and individual freedom. Those who desire to satisfy

13

their ambition to command through politics are as much to be respected as any others who also desire to command, but they must exercise their desires in fields to which political methods are applicable. Those who entertain the desire to command in material and economic things must submit themselves to the more severe and more certain tests of the market.

One of the most sinister and dangerous recent developments of this mistaken notion that political force can be applied to economic problems is to be found in the Church, where one can see the ruinous result of political action at its worst and the political idea in its most objectionable form. The parson is by nature and by right a sentimentalist, and no one would have him otherwise. Two or three weeks ago in connection with Industrial Sunday some thousands of sermons were preached by well-meaning parsons, a very large number of them failing to understand their responsibilities and echoing the stupidities of Socialist politics. The parson being a sentimentalist accepts very readily the first and the basic Socialist lie that riches are the cause of poverty, or that in any general scheme of things riches can be used to alleviate poverty. It is, of course, perfectly true that a few rich people here and there by giving £5 notes to a few poor people here and there can alleviate suffering and make life more tolerable for the few poor people. But that is only possible in this limited way, and it is profoundly untrue to suppose that any general transference of riches from the wealthy to the poor can ever be made or that any such action can ever be attempted without increasing poverty and enlarging our difficulties.

The parson accepts the Socialist lie very naturally because it is his duty to preach against the abuse of riches, but he overlooks the fact that riches can be abused in the hands of the State just as well as in the hands of the private owner. If the parsons as a whole could be made to understand that it is their duty to preach wisdom to the rich, always remembering that wealth and riches are the essential foundation of economic health, Industrial Sunday would be indeed a blessing to the nation, but the churches must be careful that they do not fall into the error of seeking favour with the mob and borrowing the envy, malice and hatred which is the stock in trade of the Socialist.

I heard a parson on the wireless preaching about wages and complaining that somebody's wages were only 28/- a week. He claimed, and as I think claimed rightly, that no wage less than £3 for a man with a family was adequate in these times. But this good man simply did not begin to understand what he was talking about. His whole mind was working in terms of money. It never dawned upon him that poverty is the absence of things, and that the only cure for poverty is to make more things. Such poverty as exists amongst us exists because the things that would remove it are non-existent, and no fundamental difference would be made to the situation if the pockets of every pauper in the land were stuffed full of the bits of paper which we call money.

I have heard many parsons rail at landlords. In every case, although, of course, my experience is limited, these sermons were built upon the assumption that all the tenants were angels.

Here is another suggestion which I would make in extension of the charge against the Church of accepting too readily everything they hear from the Socialist politician. Nobody can deny that some proportion, if not a large proportion, of the slum and housing problem is due to the inability of most people to keep any sort of house at all. I don't know how many days in the year most parsons give over to preaching sermons with Martha as a text, but if a little of the thought which is turned into invective against landlords were devoted to the study and exposition of the methods of Martha, a very big step forward would be taken to the solution of the housing problem.

There is yet another way of arguing this vital question of the application of political power to economic questions, and it seems to me a very conclusive way of showing the futility of the method as a whole. Whenever political power is applied to an economic problem, it always produces the opposite to the result desired. That may be thought by some to be too sweeping a statement, but I have yet to discover a case where any other result has developed. In connection with employment, the Ministry of Labour is established to find us jobs, and remains with us to look after unemployment.

In connection with housing, a Ministry is given powers to build us houses, with the result, as my readers have already seen, that the personnel of the building trade has been halved, and the building owner, the building investor, the building promoter, have completely disappeared. The application of political power to the mining industry, the earliest and the favourite plaything of Parliament, has brought disaster which is patent to all.

We have yet to experience the full inconveniences which are developing amongst us on account of the interference of the politicians in the matter of our food, but we, the best-fed nation in the world, are in grave danger of dropping down the scale owing to the antics of the Food Council. The endeavours of Government to get into shipping are a standing proof of the inherent impossibility of the idea of a nationalised industry, all of which brings us back to the inescapable conclusion that political control must be confined to political purposes, and that our material well-being, our economic health, our wealth-making, must be left to the free play of economic forces, through which alone the public can secure any guarantee of service or supply.

CHAPTER XVII

PRIVATE WEALTH AND PUBLIC INTEREST

There are many people outside the ranks of the Socialists who are troubled in their minds as to the justice of private wealth. There is quite enough obvious abuse of wealth to promote widespread sympathy with the idea of public ownership.

" Wealth," says John Stuart Mill, " consists of all things useful and agreeable *having exchange value*," and it is advisable to bear this definition in mind in thinking of property and its ownership, and to remember that there are various sorts of wealth. In this discussion we are only concerned with wealth as defined by John Stuart Mill. There is wealth in St. Paul's Cathedral or the Tower Bridge; there is wealth in the roads and the sewers; there is wealth of another kind in Health and Education, but none of these things was in the mind of Mill when he gave us the definition that I have quoted.

It is advisable to classify and keep separate different kinds of wealth. There is, for instance, no economic connection or similarity between the watch that is in my pocket and the fabric of Westminster Abbey. One has exchange value, and the other has no value whatever in any market where things are exchanged. A good deal of confusion arises from failure to make these classifications of wealth, confusion which is very commonly seen in the conversation of Socialists who will quote the roads and the public parks as illustrations to show that the State can own and manage factories and steamships.

Another introductory note which is necessary in

the proper consideration of the subject of wealth has to do with its comparative nature. Wealth is a matter of comparison; indeed, everything in life is comparative. Queen Elizabeth, without a water supply, and with a tallow candle as her only means of enjoying the evening hours, was a positive slum-dweller by comparison with the residents of Putney to-day. The possession of riches, property, or wealth as commonly understood consists in the possession of something that is not owned by the average person. If, for instance, everyone were reduced to a level, and everything were equally divided, there would be no wealth in the sense in which the word is often used to-day.

We mean, when we speak of wealth, the possessions of someone who owns or has control of commodities or advantages which are not available to the average person, and here we come up against one of the inherent difficulties in the democratic system, for democracy aims at spreading power equally amongst us.

In a democratic State, through the machinery of the ballot-box, every citizen possesses an equal amount of power, whereas wealth in the sense mentioned above is, and always must be, an attribute of the minority. In one way it is a difficulty; in another way it is a safeguard; in a perfectly wise State it is a very happy position when power is equally divided, but wealth remains in the hands of those who, tested by competition, are the best qualified to make, to hold and to preserve it.

This comparative characteristic of wealth is all too

little understood and considered. History, especially the history of the last 150 years, is full of examples of large masses of wealth which have been thrown into the common pool, and, because they have been divided up among us, are not recognised as wealth at all. All the marvels in engineering in the matter of transport, the provision of facilities for getting about which have enabled this generation to run from one end of London to the other, have distributed real wealth beyond the wildest dreams of our grandfathers or even fathers. When the day arrives—and it cannot be far distant—when every labourer has some sort of motor car, motor transport will cease to be wealth, and the agitation will move on to the unfortunate owners of airships. The Socialist-minded will not then question the right to a motor car any more than they now question the right to a wireless set, and all the argument about confiscation and taxation will move on to airships.

It is extremely natural for a poor man to want to divide with a rich man. It is undeniably true that if a penniless man could share up with a neighbour who has £100,000 in the bank, the former would be £50,000 better off, and here we come up against perhaps the greatest difficulty of all in all this discussion.

It is so hard for an impecunious individual with his day-by-day problems, trying to make the shillings pan out, to realise that the dividing method will not help us. The individual Socialist voter no doubt casts his vote because he thinks that in that way he will get at the individual owner of wealth; but he

forgets that we are concerned not with particular individuals, but with 43,000,000 human beings when
we consider this problem as it affects society as a
whole. The dividing folly was completely exposed
by Professor Bowley and Sir Josiah Stamp even before the war, when we were better off than we are
to-day. These distinguished statisticians proved,
and their evidence has been universally accepted by
all who have studied the question, that the Rowntree
minimum of 35s. 3d. for a man and 20s. for a
woman simply did not exist in the whole of the
national income before the war. The case, however, was really very much worse than Professor
Bowley made out, because he, as he was bound to
do, divided up the wealth of the country reckoned
in terms of money, and ignored the obvious fact that
a very great deal of that wealth, though capable of
measurement in terms of money, is from its nature
totally incapable of any physical division at all.

This brings us back to the Mill definition, and the
vital last three words "having exchange value."
A diamond may be said to be worth £10,000, and is
reckoned in the Bowley figures on that basis, but if
everybody had the 35s. 3d. a week with which those
figures were concerned, a diamond would be worth
nothing at all. Nobody could possibly pay
£10,000 for a diamond. We only say that a diamond is worth £10,000 because, as things are
arranged at the moment, there are a few people who
are capable of handing from one to another £10,000
in money in exchange for a diamond. Similarly,
property like the "Alice in Wonderland" manu-

script, sold the other day for £16,000, or my portrait by Sir William Orpen, valued at £2,000, or a stall at a theatre, valued at 14s., all disappear as wealth in the Mill sense the moment that you attempt any dividing.

There is a very great deal of work to be done in the education of the public on this simple point alone, and if it could be commonly understood that most of the wealth of which we talk is incapable of division and ceases to be wealth for Socialist purposes so soon as division is contemplated, a great deal of ground would be cleared.   As a general proposition it may be said that there are very few things possessed by the wealthy, which would be of any use at all in any system of society except the system of private ownership and personal property.   It is not suggested that the wealthy have more than their share of food; the reverse is in fact the case. The food which keeps together the body and soul of the average duke, would be quite insufficient to perform the same service for the average labourer. The wealthy classes may perhaps possess a superabundance of clothing and some of them might be able to part with a few suits or a few dresses, but there is for the most part very little else which could be used in any scheme for dividing wealth more equally.   The Rolls Royce can never be divided. It would be easy to take one man out of a Rolls Royce and put him in the gutter and take another man out of the gutter and put him into the Rolls Royce, but that would not be the division of wealth; it would be merely the substitution of one situation for another. If only we could get people into the habit of thinking in things instead of money, if it were recognised that poverty is the absence of things, and that wealth is the possession of things or the power over them, a great deal of misapprehension would be avoided. It is difficult, very difficult, it always will be difficult, so long as we desire to enjoy the advantages of a convenient medium of exchange like money. The more we develop the machinery of money, the more difficult it will become, and the more necessary, therefore, is it for everybody to understand that money is nothing but a tally, a means of reckoning, a medium of exchange, and has no other use, purpose or value.

The driving force behind the idea of the division or the better distribution of wealth is the notion that riches are the cause of poverty, a wholly false idea. When you add to this fallacy all that natural weakness from which very few of us are free and which makes us feel a certain envy of those who do better than ourselves, you have the complete explanation, not only of the Socialist movement, but of the movement in all political parties for higher taxation and more public expenditure.

When Parliament has to consider another shilling on the super tax or another addition to the death duties, it is safe to say that while some of the members are thinking entirely of the need for the money and the purpose to which it will be put, the majority is formed of those who feel that the super tax payer and the wealthy testator are fair game for punishment.

Riches are the antidote to poverty, not the cause of it. Poverty is the absence of riches, and more poverty is made by preventing the acquisition of new riches or the retention of old. The man or woman who succeeds by any proper means in the difficult task of acquiring some new riches does not in point of fact deprive anybody else of those riches. What he or she does is to contribute towards the setting of new standards which in time become the common standards. The ordinary amenities of life now common to everybody, sanitation, clothes, food, means of transport, literature, were each in their time highly-prized wealth, owned and enjoyed by the privileged few. The study of any market emphasises this point. In clothes the fashion is set by Worth or Paquin, is enjoyed for a brief spell by a wealthy minority, and in an incredibly short space of time is available to the whole of the civilised world. These things happen very quickly in clothes, but they happen just as surely in everything else.

The first lady's safety bicycle that I can remember was made by the Enfield Company in the early nineties and cost £35. In the village where I then lived this bicycle caused a good deal of heartburning among the women who, because they were not in the position of the fortunate daughter of the Squire, busied themselves with discussing the impropriety of bicycling for women and the frightful waste of £35 on such a fantastic whim. But while that particular bicycle could never have been divided, it was directly responsible for the £3 10s. od. machine which every girl can buy to-day and which would not be on the market if its £35 predecessor had been taxed out of existence. I am perfectly sure that if the Squire who gave his daughter that expensive bicycle had been subject to the present rate of taxation, the bicycle would never have been bought and probably never have been made.

There is in these days no case for ownership as mere ownership. The "what's mine's my own" line of argument is not only out of date, but dangerous, and, I think, wrong. Individualists in discussing these matters with Socialists, especially sentimental Socialists, are badly handicapped by the incontestable fact that many of the owners of wealth are not good citizens, and do not appear to be useful members of society.

The Squire's daughter with her £35 bicycle spent, if I remember rightly, far too much of her time in mere frivolity, and it would be absurd to argue that when riding her bicycle she was conscious of the tremendous economic developments in which she was a pioneer.

Private property in present circumstances can only be justified in the public interest. The owners of private property must be regarded as trustees on behalf of the public. Only on these lines can Individualism hope to make an appeal to thoughtful people. The argument must be built up in this way. Civilisation depends upon property, upon the making and saving of ever greater quantities of real wealth, and as all history proves that the private individual is the only agent that can make, preserve and save wealth, society is dependent upon the private individual as the owner of wealth.

We all depend upon saving. Life itself would disappear unless a sufficient amount of saving is done. We have only to eat the whole of this year's potato crop to be sure that no potatoes would exist next year. It is immaterial to society, who saves the seed potatoes from this year's crop. The essential thing is that they must be saved. The private individual may be actuated by the lowest motives of personal gain when he does the saving. I myself do not find those private individuals whom I know to be full of greed and avarice and personal desire in the way that we are asked to believe by Socialists. But that does not matter. The point is not a good one. Whatever may be the motive, the economic necessity is that the saving should be made.

The savings made by society in its collective capacity, by States, by County Councils, and by other public authorities are infinitesimal, and there is no single case where the real property owned by a public authority is worth more than a fraction of the debt piled up by the same agency. The individual is always striving to save, always striving to put something away for a rainy day or for a future generation.

It is an extraordinary and disturbing reflection that when this same individual becomes a member of a public body he proceeds at once to reverse his policy and to pile up debts and obligations which he leaves to future generations to discharge. It can thus be seen that there is really no such thing as public ownership. What the politicians mean when they talk that way is the use of the things which are privately owned by the individuals of the moment, and the mortgaging of the things which they hope will be owned by the individuals of the future. The list of failures of public ownership is a very long one; the list of failures of public management is equally long, and indeed nobody denies, so far as I am aware, that such industrial efforts as have been made in the name of the public, or as experiments in Socialism, have hitherto failed.

There is another line of argument which can be pursued with advantage in this connection. It does seem plausible to think that the wisdom of a government or a council is at least as great as the wisdom of the individual, and it is hard to doubt that a public body is of itself less qualified to own a coal mine than, let us say, the Duke of Northumberland. But that idea arises from a failure to understand the way in which the work of the world is really done. We all depend upon multitudinous little bits of effort pulling in all sorts of directions and conflicting one with another. Socialism seems to think that a policy can be devised for the guidance of everybody, and that we can all move forward together in one uniform progress.

The truth, surely, is that in every little detail of life a balance is necessary. That balance is maintained by conflicting interests or opposing forces. This book exists because one man wants to get rid of it and another wants to acquire it. The fact that it contains this chapter, which is an emphatic protest against the current of public opinion, is another reason among the many which bring it into existence. But the moment that any property or any enterprise is owned by the public it has to conform to a policy accepted by the whole public.

We makeshift for the moment with majority opinion, but Russia and all Socialism bank on unanimous opinion. There is no room for contradiction or conflict or a balance of forces in the Socialist philosophy, and it thus comes about that public enterprise lacks the essential essence of enterprise, and the need for uniformity reduces the whole scheme to a dead level of inefficiency. The moment that a little bit of property or a little bit of work gets into the hands of a public authority it must conform to well-understood principles and well-defined practices. Interest passes automatically from the little bit of work to the principles and practices. This is natural and necessary and is another explanation of the impossibility of the Socialist idea.

It is easy to rail at red tape, at forms, at bureaucratic methods, but these things are inseparable from public enterprise and constitute the simplest practical reason why public enterprise is impossible.

The fortune which the Duke of Northumberland is reputed to take out of coal mines may or may not be an abuse, that depends on the use which the Duke makes of the fortune, but the fact remains that public ownership of the same mines would involve expenditure in connection with the necessary imposition of principles and practice far in excess of any fortune which the most rapacious duke has ever taken out of mineral rights.

I have always felt, and still feel, that the theoretical argument for the public ownership of land is unanswerable, but then I come to this same practical difficulty. The cost of the public ownership of land, because of the necessity for the observance of uniform principles and practice, would be far heavier than all the ground rents and unearned increments of which we hear so much to-day.

Private property can thus be justified in theory as well as in practice. In practice the justification rests mainly upon the inherent impossibility of public ownership, supported by illustrations which are to be found on every hand. The amenities of life, all those material things on which we depend, all those little things of which each generation requires increasing quantities, and which pass very rapidly one after the other from the class of riches and luxury into the class of necessities, can be divided very simply into two big categories : those which have been left to private enterprise and individual ownership on the one hand, and those which have been the subject of political action on the other.

The contrast between these two categories is marked, startling and convincing. The world is well supplied with clothes, food, literature, and amusements, to name only four big simple classes. On the other hand, where the political idea has entered, where political action and collectivist theory have been applied, there is want, shortage and poverty. It is only necessary to name, in this

14

connection, houses, coal and employment. In each of these three matters the interference of the politician, the attempt to apply the powers of collectivism, have landed us in disaster.

It must also be remembered that private property is quite worthless to the private owner unless it is used in the public interest. Whether the property appears to take the form of money or whether it consists in buildings or plant or stock, the owner can only derive benefit from it by placing it on terms at the service of others. The private proprietor is constantly impelled to find new ways of inducing other people to made adequate and proper use of his property. Public ownership is in quite another position. It can leave property to rot, as in the case of Slough or Richborough, or it can use property in a way which is not acceptable to a sufficient number of people to pay expenses, and take the loss out of the successes of the private owner. When property is in public hands there is no effective test of adequate use, whereas the private owner is, for the most part, under the absolute necessity to use it in such a way as freely to attract others.

CHAPTER XVIII

THE INDIVIDUALIST AS A POLITICIAN

THE reader, so far, will have noticed that we have discussed numerous questions of current party controversy, with a freedom and irresponsibility altogether inconsistent with active loyalty to any one of the political parties.

But political parties exist and with the revival in party activity now noticeable in all directions, the Individualist has to ask himself what is his duty, what should he do, and, in particular, how is he to vote? At the Individualist Bookshop we are constantly asked whether it is our intention to run candidates, and whether there will be any attempt to found an Individualist party in the House of Commons itself. I set out our aspirations fairly clearly in the first chapter of this book in the following terms:

"The challenge of Individualism is making people think, and when the next General Election comes a very large proportion of the voters will have reached the mental stage in which they can clearly see the two alternatives which face us. Are we to continue the pitiful attempt to erect a State whose sole object is to act as wet nurse to the people, sparing them the painful necessity of doing anything for themselves, or are we to develop a people who can support and look after themselves as well as the State?"

Can these aspirations be realised without some attempt on regular political lines to establish a foothold in the House of Commons itself? There are those who argue that a cause like ours requires the backing of a party machine. It is said that no good impression can be made upon political thought or political development without the assistance of one or other of the great political parties. The elector is, in the nature of things, bound to attach himself more or less firmly to some political organisation, and so the argument runs, Individualists should have a clear lead and a definite course given to them.

But the most superficial examination shows that those who argue this way are the victims of the early workings of the microbe of Collectivism. They are labouring under that favourite political delusion, the most common of all political weaknesses, the idea that "something must be done." In the philosophy of the Individualist, however, the greatest political wisdom is generally to be found in the opposite direction, and in insisting that nothing shall be "done." Political action, described by John Morley as "a choice of second bests," is, in our view, a dangerous and disappointing weapon that should never be used until the absence of any other conceivable plan has been demonstrated beyond dispute.

Those who think that we ought to adopt a party label would have us take one of three courses, and, strange as it may seem, any one of these opposing courses is open to us. Individualists could organise themselves together and declare that they were Conservatives, Liberals or Labour, for such is the flabbiness and emptiness of party politics to-day that

any of these parties would welcome the introduction
of anything so vigorous, so helpful, so sane as the
gospel which we preach if they could have it to
themselves. Many Conservatives assure me that
their party is enthusiastically with us, and if only we
Individualists would put our weight into it we could
silence that latter-day curiosity, the Tory-Socialist,
and bring the party back to economy, self help, and
non-interference. Similarly, there is a large body
of Liberal opinion which is altogether of our way
of thinking, and I do not doubt that if the whole
force of the Individualists were applied to the cause
of Liberalism that great party could be restored to
those principles upon which it was founded, and
could be saved from the clutches of the synthetic
Socialists who, for the moment, appear to have
secured control of it.

There is a third course open to us; one, strange
to say, that appeals to me much more strongly. We
could join the Labour party and turn it into a real
Labour party, as distinguished from a Socialist or
Communist party. This is not at all an impossible
job; indeed, there is nothing more certain in politics
at all than the return of the trade union movement
to a constructive as distinguished from a destructive
industrial policy. The reception given to my little
book, *If I Were a Labour Leader*, has more
than justified this prophecy, and the welcome ac-
corded to the ideas which I there attempted to
develop shows the strength of Individualism even
in the most unexpected quarters. The average
labouring man wants to get on with the job of

abolishing poverty, and he knows that trade unionism run in the interests of industry and production is a very different thing from political Socialism. That is why half the wage-earners never vote for a Socialist candidate and never will.

But if Individualists as a class took any one of these three courses and entered the arena of party combat they would assuredly weaken their powers for usefulness. We should make one friend and two enemies whichever course we took. The moment we call ourselves Blue all the Yellows and the Reds are against us; such is the tyranny of the party machine. If we elect to be Yellow the Blues and the Reds declare war upon us, and that is the one great disadvantage of the party method from our point of view. We have a higher purpose, a nobler mission, a more definitely useful work to do. We can exercise a widespread influence upon public opinion as a whole. We can carry on an educational mission in all parties, and in that way establish a basis of sound public opinion on which party politics can operate with less damage to the commonweal than is possible at the moment.

I am not objecting to the opposition of the Reds and the Blues. Opposition, discussion, dispute, argument are all necessary to get a balance and a judgment into public affairs. If the Home Secretary appoints a Commission to inquire into the Savidge case, and arranges for it to meet the following day, it is important that the Opposition should point out with emphasis the dangers of this unseemly speed. If, on the other hand, the Home

Secretary arranges for the Commission to do its work in a more orderly and judicial manner, it is equally important that the Opposition should lash itself into fury at the intolerable delay.

This illustration from the detail of the Savidge case illustrates political method generally, and political method for party purposes is right and good. Each political party seems to think it necessary to have a housing policy, and whatever that policy may be, whatever its details, whether, indeed, they are even known or not, the other two parties will declare the whole thing to be bad, ill conceived, unworkable and wrong. Exactly the same thing happens with mines, or pensions, or taxation, or anything that a political party handles. The Labour party stumped the country to denounce the trade union policy of the Conservatives, and in the most blatant, though perfectly proper political way, made it clear that, whatever the policy turned out to be when later the Prime Minister announced it, they would offer it the most strenuous opposition.

When this sort of thing comes down to economic detail, party politics degenerates into the most degrading auction. Thus, if the Conservatives offer a pension of 5s., the Liberals say it should be 10s., and the Socialists claim that they will give a sovereign. All this is proper politics. We must have a Government, and we must have His Majesty's Opposition. These are the safeguards, the finishing touches of political life, but they are not the whole of life. Individualism is something deeper, more fundamental, more necessary, and

Individualism must not weaken or degrade itself by association with party strife.

The right method for the Individualist is the Gompers method. If we were operating in America instead of more sober Britain, we should probably adopt some expressive slogan like "To Hell with Politics." Such a slogan would not be fair (but slogans never are), because we are, of course, the real politicians, we are concerned with the well-being of the whole body politic, and we must be free from the necessity of vote catching and place seeking. There is nothing in the whole world in the shape of real political success to approach the position of the American working man. That position was secured by Samuel Gompers, who for forty years led the American Federation of Labour and kept it right outside established party limits.

"Only once have I ever been a member of a political party," says Gompers in his *Seventy Years of Life and Labour.* "When I became of age I joined the Republican organisation in the district in which I lived. To me it was an organisation which still had a great purpose to fulfil. Lincoln typified that purpose in my mind. . . . When I left the Republican party I joined no other. . . . It will be observed that in recent years I have voted for the Presidential candidate on the Democratic ticket, and this has been interpreted by many to mean that I am a member of the Democratic party. . . . As I have already stated, in the first four years of my citizenship I was a member of the Republican party. For years after in Presidential elections I cast a protesting vote. I believe that the Republican party had fulfilled its mission, growing out of the Civil War, and so far as the Democratic party was concerned it had no concept of the political and industrial problems of the times.

" Anyone who will doubt the sincerity of the non-partisan policy which I have endeavoured to pursue may compare the platform declarations of the Democratic and Republican parties and judge for himself whether I was not justified as a Labour man. . . . I have always sought to use political situations for Labour's advantage."

All parties in America paid their respect to Samuel Gompers; all of them competed to serve the cause of Labour which he represented. He declined absolutely to have a party of his own, or to be associated with any party. He steered this difficult course with such success that there is to-day about as much chance for a Socialist party in America as for the Strict Baptists in the Sahara Desert.

In the short time that the Individualists have been a vocal force operating from the little bookshop in Charing Cross Road, we have demonstrated the advantages to be gained from a non-party policy. We have had the privilege of entertaining on our platform leading thinkers from every party, and from circles where politics count for nothing.

The proper attitude of the Individualist to party politics is not unlike the proper attitude of the Churchman. The Church exists, or, in my judgment, it should exist, to exercise an influence on every aspect of life, politics included.   The Church should welcome members of every political party, but should stand aloof from party controversy, and rely upon the principles which it exists to inculcate, to influence party controversy for good.

My advice, therefore, to Individualists is to keep within any party where they can find a sufficient measure of sympathy to make their presence welcome to others and comfortable to themselves. They should strive to keep the party straight from their point of view, and to restrain the natural movement of every party towards further developments of State action at the expense of the Individual. When the time comes to vote I shall support the candidate who will undertake to " do " the least, who will offer the smallest bribes to the electors, and who will promise to restrain the mad modern rush for wealth and happiness through legislation.   If a candidate is to be found with the pluck to tell the electors the real truth, and Mr. Baldwin comes remarkably near to it now and again, I shall take off my coat and work and fight for him.

Such a candidate would go to the polls with an address framed in something like the following terms:

To the electors of London or Rome.   Ladies and Gentlemen, I ask your support at the forthcoming election as an Individualist.   I am firmly of the opinion that the craze for Government has been overdone, and that the need of the country to-day is for less Government, not more.   I view with the gravest alarm the ever-increasing tendency of large masses of the people to look for State help, not only in the form of doles for the poor, but of subsidies and reliefs for the rich.   I believe the economic power of the State to be very limited, and the power of the Individual to be capable of indefinite expansion.   The candidate who tells you that the State can feed and clothe and house its citizens is lying. If we have a prosperous State composed of prosperous Individuals these things can be done for the small minority which fails, but that is the limit of the possibilities of political or State action.   I therefore offer you nothing, promise you nothing and I call on you as good citizens to strive to strengthen your personal positions and thus strengthen the State.

If you make a personal success of life I will, as a member of Parliament, vote a part of that success, in the name of charity and good social policy, for the support of those who fail.   I denounce as false, degrading, and anti-social the notion that failure can confer any rights.   Success, to be complete, embodies the obligation to help failure, but failure does not carry with it the right to share success. Life is a personal thing.   The power to strive, the obligation to serve and the responsibility to move forwards or backwards on your road whatever it may be, are all personal to you alone and single-handed.   You have few rights, but many duties. Through the collective machinery of politics, civilisation has developed certain political rights. The State can give you political liberty, the right to talk and think, the right to peace and quiet, the right to knowledge, if you have the personal capacity to contain it, but the State can give you very little else. For the rest it is up to you.

I claim to represent all that is most worthy in our national life, a life which will prosper or decay in proportion to our acceptance or rejection of the gospel of Individualism. On these grounds I ask for your support.

Your obedient servant,

The Individualist.

There is nothing in all this which can be described as practical politics, there is not a shred of vote-catching about it. It ignores altogether the possibility of some party or another winning some particular election on some particular crisis. It dismisses as mere detail most of the matters of day-by-day controversy, but it does bring politics back to principles, and that is surely what is really wanted.

For fifty years laisser faire has been discarded as a national policy and to-day the term is not only derided and misunderstood but deliberately misrepresented. Many people even think the words mean " leave alone " and give to the policy a negative or " don't care " implication. Laisser faire means, of course, " let do," " leave to do," do not interfere with action, and as all action comes from the individual the denial of the policy of laisser faire has robbed us of a tremendous and beneficent mass of action, which had it taken place, would have kept this country the happiest and wealthiest place in the world.

If England recovers its Individualism, it will scorn the helpless, dependent, pauper-like frame of mind which present-day politics has created, and all political parties will be obliged to mend their ways.

Individualists, as such, therefore, will know no party; they have the higher duty of providing a wise, truthful, philosophical, and intellectual basis on which detailed political controversy at any given moment can operate with much more promise of good and safety than is possible in the present state of party politics.

If England recovers its Individualism, it will
scorn the helpless, dependent, pauper-like frame of
mind which present-day politics has created, and all
political parties will be obliged to amend their ways.
Individualists, as such, therefore, will know no
party; they have the higher duty of providing a
wise, truthful, philosophical, and intellectual basis
on which detailed political controversy at any given
moment can operate with much more promise of
good and safety than is possible in the present state
of party politics.